# Reducing Stress-related Behaviours
# in People with Dementia

*of related interest*

**The Simplicity of Dementia**
**A Guide for Family and Carers**
*Huub Buijssen*
ISBN 1 84310 321 4

**Understanding Dementia**
**The Man with the Worried Eyes**
*Richard Cheston and Michael Bender*
ISBN 1 85302 479 1

**A Guide to the Spiritual Dimension of Care for People**
**with Alzheimer's Disease and Related Dementia**
**More than Body, Brain and Breath**
*Eileen Shamy*
*Forewords by Richard Sainsbury, Robert Baldwin and Albert Jewell*
ISBN 1 84310 129 7

**Hearing the Voice of People with Dementia**
**Opportunities and Obstacles**
*Malcolm Goldsmith*
*Preface by Mary Marshall*
ISBN 1 85302 406 6

**Dancing with Dementia**
**My Story of Living Positively with Dementia**
*Christine Bryden*
ISBN 1 84310 332 X

**Perspectives on Rehabilitation and Dementia**
*Edited by Mary Marshall*
ISBN 1 84310 286 2

# Reducing Stress-related Behaviours in People with Dementia

## Care-based therapy

*Chris Bonner*

*Illustrated by Wayne Madden*

Jessica Kingsley Publishers
London and Philadelphia

First published in 2005
by Jessica Kingsley Publishers
116 Pentonville Road
London N1 9JB, UK
and
400 Market Street, Suite 400
Philadelphia, PA 19106, USA

*www.jkp.com*

**Library of Congress Cataloging in Publication Data**
A CIP catalog record for this book is available from the Library of Congress

**British Library Cataloguing in Publication Data**
A CIP catalogue record for this book is available from the British Library

ISBN-13: 978 1 84310 349 3
ISBN-10: 1 84310 349 4

Printed and Bound in Great Britain by
Athenaeum Press, Gateshead, Tyne and Wear

# Contents

# Acknowledgements

I wish to acknowledge the contribution of care staff and residents from the 26 care facilities for which I am a consultant, and others who have contributed to the content of this manual. Specifically I thank those who waded through every word, and responded with some excellent thoughts. I also acknowledge Prue Mellor of Age Concern, Australia, who has contributed to my enthusiasm of the subject as well as contributing wise insights in her courses on the care of people with dementia.

Finally I acknowledge my wife Marelle's support for my work and the inspiration gleaned from her uncanny and intuitive understanding of the needs of her own mother, who has dementia.

*Chris Bonner*

# Introduction

This manual draws information from the literature, the numerous carers with whom I have worked, and personal experience in caring for and enjoying the company of people with dementia. It focuses on the concept of a progressively lowered stress threshold in Alzheimer's disease (Hall 1994). The concept specifically addresses Alzheimer's disease, the most common form of dementia. Issues relating to this concept may be particularly appropriate to Alzheimer's disease, but may also be applicable to other causes of dementia.

The fact that I am a clinical pharmacist authoring a book on the care of people with dementia may seem a little unusual, but I was initially motivated by my concern regarding the devastating effects of some medications traditionally used to modify behaviour in people with dementia. Not that drug therapy is contraindicated for this purpose in dementia. It needs, however, to be considered carefully, and appropriate care practices can dramatically reduce the reliance on psychotropic medications (Shelkey and Lantz 1998). If this manual makes sense despite my pharmacological perspective, all I can say is that the numerous carers I have worked with over the years have taught me well.

Many of the care initiatives offered in this manual are validated by research. Others are no more than suggestions. Some of the information may even be contradictory. Validated information means that we can expect the information to be appropriate in a significant number of settings. Suggestions mean that someone considers a certain practice might be effective, but the significance of the practice in improving overall care is unknown.

In caring for people with dementia, so much is unknown. Research funds earmarked for dementia tend to be directed towards finding a cure or developing medications to slow down the disease process or the effects of the disease. It is easier to find evidence about the behavioural characteristics of people with dementia and the effects of various interventions than to find out how people with dementia are likely to feel emotionally. Many authors have proposed excellent concepts for understanding the world of the person with dementia, but even so we need to look at each person and situation individually rather than base our care relationships on collective theories or notions. There is no test or protocol as there often is in medicine to tell us what to do. Therefore, our efforts to improve outcomes for people with dementia will require knowledge, empathy, careful assessment, and patiently experimenting with a range of interventions designed to remove any underlying cause or stress and produce the best outcomes. Whether the approach is validated, or merely a case report, or is intuitive, what matters is what works for any particular person. The aim of this manual is to gather together as many ideas as possible from a wide variety of sources. We must of course avoid practices that are accompanied by risk. We must discard what does not work, build on what works and communicate what works to all involved in the care of the person with dementia.

This manual is primarily directed towards carers in residential aged-care facilities, but the concepts can be applied to care in the domestic home by family members and other carers. A carer in this manual means anyone involved in care: domestic personnel, hands-on care staff, doctors, volunteers, nurses, administrators, friends, pharmacists. We usually refer to those we care for in residential aged-care facilities as 'residents'. However, in this manual, the term can be taken to include those being cared for at home.

It is hoped that you will find great satisfaction as you enter the world of the person with dementia to provide care which focuses on that person, a person who is unique and with a rich range of feelings and emotions to appreciate and enjoy. It is hoped that, in your work, new care ideas will emerge and eventually be shared with others through resources such as this manual.

# 1

# Stress factors

The development of dementia causes cognitive loss (loss of mental processes of comprehension, judgement, memory and reasoning) and conative loss (involving changes in behaviour and actions) in many cases perceived as personality changes. Stress-related behaviours, often referred to as Behavioural and Psychological Symptoms of Dementia (BPSD), commonly emerge as the condition progresses and, besides being a burden to the sufferer, can be distressing for carers (Hart *et al.* 2003). These behaviours may be the result of a progressively lowered threshold to stress (Hall 1994) or 'shrinking of the comfort zone' (Caron and Goetz 1998) resulting in stress-related responses such as agitation and aggression. Triggers such as loss of family and friends, a comprehensible environment, decision-making responsibility, physical ability, affiliations and freedom increase susceptibility to these stress-related behaviours.

Short-term memory is usually lost first, while long-term memory is retained. Thus people with dementia may find present places, faces and practices unfamiliar and stressful. They may feel as if they are surrounded by strangers.

Pre-existing pathological conditions, personalities or character styles, or neurochemical or structural abnormalities in the brain, may underlie stress-related responses in people with dementia (Dyck 1997). Depression is more common in people with dementia than in non-demented people and this may result in their being more emotionally vulnerable to stress (Verhey and Visser 2000). These factors in association with cognitive impairment reduce tolerance to adverse environmental stimuli (such as unfamiliar routines, care practices or environments) (Raskind 1999).

Common stressors that may overwhelm a person's reduced coping threshold include:

- mental and physical fatigue

- change of daily routine, caregiver or surroundings

- misleading stimuli or inappropriate stimulus levels

- excessive internal or external demands to achieve beyond their functional capacity

- physical stressors such as pain or physical irritation, infection, dehydration or depression

- affective response to perceived functional losses of day-to-day skills and independence

- loss of ability to communicate needs and comprehend spoken words.

(Hall 1994; Hall and Buckwater 1991)

People with dementia can be frightened or anxious when exposed to stressors. Their capacity to cope can be easily exceeded in a situation of failure (Hall, Kirschling and Todd 1986).

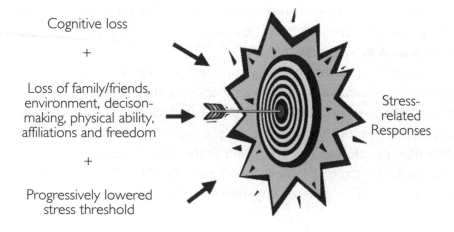

Cognitive loss

+

Loss of family/friends, environment, decison-making, physical ability, affiliations and freedom

+

Progressively lowered stress threshold

Stress-related Responses

The losses associated with dementia may be further compounded by 'excess disabilities': the presentation of reversible symptoms of functional incapacity greater than warranted by physiological impairments. Excess disability may result from unrecognized or inadequately treated medical conditions, medications, or various emotional, psychological and environmental factors. Medical burden is of course a source of excess disability but sensory loss due to unsuitable spectacles or wax impaction of the ears can lead to decreased cognition, hallucinations, delusions, emotional lability, isolation and agitation (Morley and Miller 1993). Medication side-effects can produce unnecessary disability, and care techniques that assist the person to perform tasks which they would still be capable of performing for themselves (albeit slowly) can lead to excess dependency for activities of daily living. Environmental complexity resulting in difficulty accessing the toilet can promote unnecessary incontinence. Muscles that are not used may deteriorate.

Imagine your reactions to the following situations.

> You are driving the family to see your spouse's parents. You have other things you would prefer to do. In fact the only time a trip to visit the parents-in-law in Italy could be arranged happened to be the week of the annual fishing trip, which you haven't missed for ten years. You are jet-lagged, have a headache, can't stand driving a Fiat, it's turned dark and you cannot see or read the road signs. In fact you are lost, and the kids are conducting a war in the back seat. Still you are keeping your cool...just. Then your adorable teenage daughter indulges in a truce with her brothers for long enough to say, 'I bet you forgot to bring the present for grandma.' That was an odds-on bet, so you now add a feeling of disrespect and failure to your stress and frustration.

## You would probably cope better with this situation:

> You have had a good day. You are celebrating a success by buying yourself that special perfume. As you stand at the counter savouring the moment, a passer-by gives you a little push or bump to get through a congested aisle. You probably cope with this well.

Now let's look at the same event under different circumstances:

> You have had a really bad day; you lost your job, the pet dog is missing and you have dented your car. You are buying a gift that you can ill afford for an aunt you don't particularly like but are obliged to honour appropriately.

How do you feel now when pushed by the impatient person? Is your stress threshold or tolerance reduced?

## Results of stress

Naturally stress will result in overall poor health outcomes, agitation, a reduced ability to attend to activities of daily living, and will make care more difficult and less pleasant.

Billing (1996) indicates that stress can also lead to:

- physically aggressive behaviour such as hitting, scratching, spitting or biting

- verbally aggressive behaviour such as abuse or cursing

- physically non-aggressive behaviour such as inappropriate disrobing, wandering or intrusiveness

- verbally non-aggressive behaviour such as yelling, incessant demands or constantly repeating words or remarks.

A person with dementia may live with frustrations, losses and reduced tolerances, and consistently be adversely affected by seemingly minor or imagined insults or stresses. That can be the world of the person with dementia. People with dementia need care that finds and accounts for what they want to do, cures the headache, minimizes disruption, simplifies life for them, avoids fatigue, interprets the environment, respects them and doesn't challenge them or ask silly questions.

Feeding and sleeping problems, although not necessarily stress-related, may also be evident in people with dementia, and be a challenge to manage.

2

# Preventing/minimizing stress

Providing the best care for people with dementia exhibiting stress begins with a thorough assessment to search for underlying causes of behaviour change. Concomitant medical illness should be treated and sensory impairment addressed. Assessment and management are essential components of the treatment of dementia (Herrmann 2001).

## Find out as much as you can about the person

As long-term memory is preserved longer than short-term memory in dementia, the world as seen in the mind of the person with dementia will often be in the distant past. Thus care practices need to be based on an intimate knowledge of the person's life. We also need an accurate picture of how the  person is functioning at significant points in time, such as on admission to residential care. Establishing a baseline is also important so that we can objectively validate the outcomes of care practices.

### Establish a baseline of function

On admission to residential care, it is important to assess cognition, mood, performance of activities of daily living, mobility and general function. For people being cared for at home, a community nurse or a doctor, possibly by referral, could gain this information.

- Conduct baseline tests of cognitive status such as the Mini-Mental State Exam (MMSE) (Folstein, Folstein and McHugh 1975), which provides a score out of 30 to assess memory, orientation (knowledge of time and place), comprehension, attention (ability to maintain focus), command of language visuospatial skills (ability to process and interpret visual information about where objects are in space) and motor skills.

- Assess mood. Various geriatric depression scales are available and may be suitable for some patients. However, depression may fluctuate, the patient may be 'stoic' or answers may be affected by cognitive loss and result in responses that underestimate the likelihood of depression. If this is suspected to be the case, gain information from someone close to the person (Rubin *et al.* 2001) and document mood in the interview and in the performance of the mental states examination. Depression in elderly individuals is associated with reduced cognitive test performance, especially in more complex and time-demanding tests and tests of memory (Palsson *et al.* 2000).

- Document general presentation, level of awareness, attitude to the interviewer, ability to understand and communicate information and whether thought processes are logical. Besides word-finding abilities, people with dementia may also have an impaired ability to receive information logically.

- Check if the person has insight into their disability. Those who have insight may be more prone to depression, whereas those without may be more prone to paranoid ideation.

- Assess mobility, postural stability and for the presence of any movement disorders. A range of standardized tests is available to assess physical function.

- Assess ability to perform activities of daily living, continence and sleep patterns.

- Ask about personal concerns.

- Check if the person suffers from hallucinations, delusions, obsessions or compulsions.

- Where specific stress-related or agitated behaviours are evident use a behaviour chart to describe and document baseline behaviour. A behaviour chart improves consistency in assessment and provides credible information to judge the effectiveness of interventions and assist in decision-making. Confirm that such behaviour is persistent or occasional.

## Assess medical status

Although this is primarily the role of medical practice, care staff at all levels are involved in monitoring and reporting symptoms for professional assessment. Care personnel will often be in a position to advocate the medical needs of the patient to determine the cause of any emerging symptoms.

People exhibiting agitated behaviours in dementia warrant a full medical and psychiatric assessment for the following:

- Depression – can underlie agitated behaviours in people with dementia and such people should be assessed for depression and treated if necessary (Menon et al. 2001). Although care-based therapy will be first-line therapy in treating depression, a careful trial of antidepressant medication will often be appropriate and beneficial.

- Delusions, hallucinations – stress-related disturbances may be associated with delusions or hallucinations. Delusions are an unshakable belief in something untrue. In dementia they may often present as a false belief related to cognitive deficits, such as the belief that a deceased parent is alive. In other more distressing cases delusions may involve distorted ideas about what is actually happening. This may involve a belief that their home is not their own, that a close relative has been replaced by an impostor or that their belongings are being stolen. Besides seeing, or hearing things that are not there, hallucinations can involve smelling, tasting or feeling things which are not there. Misinterpretations, such as believing a stripe on a carpet is a snake, are distinct from hallucinations and can trouble people with dementia. It has been claimed that delusions commonly appear after five years of dementing illness and at an MMSE of 12 (Deutsch and Rovner 1991), representing moderate to advanced dementia.

- Delirium – this usually involves a diminished ability to pay attention, confusion, disorientation and an inability to think clearly, and can present as a hyper- or hypoactive disorder in the elderly. Delirium is often due to an underlying illness and is potentially reversible. Many elderly people with dementia may have coexisting delirium, which is not necessarily transient. Common causes of delirium include infections; endocrine disorders (hyper- or hypoglycaemia); decreased cardiac output due to heart conditions; poor oxygen availability due to respiratory problems or anaemia; dehydration; transient ischaemic attacks; medications; hyper- or hypothermia; changes in environment; constipation or urinary retention (Espino et al. 1998).

- Deficits in hearing and vision – these can lead to perceptual distortion.

- Disorder determined by biochemical tests – electrolyte or liver function abnormalities; endocrine disorders such as diabetes, overactive or underactive thyroid; deficiences in vitamin B12, folate or vitamin D; syphilis; urinary tract infections; inflammatory disorders.

- Haematological abnormalities – such as anaemia.

- Pain, physical discomfort or irritation – for example from itch or vaginitis.

- Constipation.

- Infection.

- Transient ischaemic attacks or seizures.

- Adverse effects of medications.

Although usually unavailable, knowledge of the specific or predominant type of dementia (e.g. Alzheimer's, multi-infarct, Lewy body, fronto-temporal) is useful in predicting behaviours and interventions. For instance, people with Lewy Body dementia can suffer severe reactions to antipsychotic drugs and these drugs must be avoided when there is any suspicion of this condition. People with fronto-temporal dementia will often do well on cognitive testing, despite their dementia being advanced to the extent that they can no longer safely care for themselves.

---

After a seminar on depression, the hostel supervisor remarked that the person cleaning Mrs Smith's room had noticed her becoming more immobile and 'flat' over the last month. It was suggested she might be depressed. It turned out that the immobility and 'flat' appearance was due to an antipsychotic prescribed for delusions. On further investigation the delusions appeared subsequent to an intimate care procedure for which a less intimate procedure was available. The person cleaning Mrs Smith's room prevented major disability by being a thinking person in the care team.

---

Patients with a complex psychiatric or cognitive presentation may benefit from psychogeriatric or neuropsychological assessment. Such assessment clarifies diagnosis, assesses cognitive abilities in several domains, identifies behaviours and behavioural changes and provides recommendations for future care (Peterson and Lantz 2001). Many city hospitals have geriatric units, including Geriatric Outreach Teams, available to conduct the necessary assessments.

## *Assess social and occupational history*

Assess social, occupational, cultural and spiritual history and use this information in care practices. This may involve a detailed interview with the person and a close associate, familiar with the person's day-to-day function. Learn what is special about each of your residents and try to respond accordingly.

- Obtain a written snapshot of their life history, activities, social relationships, cultural practices, religious beliefs, spiritual needs and war service. Negative aspects of one's life history may well surface as a significant stressor in association with cognitive impairment and difficulty in interpreting their circumstances. Ask about educational achievements and career. Check how they spent their day, their habits, likes and dislikes, what they like to talk about, whether they like to be alone or in company, their food preferences and their colour preferences. Gaining this information before admission to a residential aged care facility will allow care approaches to maximize individual expression and need for fulfilment, reduce stress and enhance function. Recovering access to familiar, enjoyable or meaningful practices may be important in maintaining quality of life. Something as simple as folding laundry items may prove a meaningful link to the past for some elderly people with dementia.

- Source information on interests, activities and levels of social participation. Identify strengths and weaknesses.

- Document any traumatic life events or abuse that become known. Although it may not be appropriate to actively source this information, any such events are likely to be particularly significant as underlying causes of distress in a person with dementia. Such events could have been traumatic and may have remained unreported and unresolved.

One senior nurse-educator makes the point that she becomes very frustrated when she listens to eulogies at funerals of deceased residents, when these eulogies contain significant information that, if available while the person was alive, would have assisted in caring for them.

There may be an association between preceding or premorbid personality and behaviour in dementia (Low *et al.* 2002). Gaining information on premorbid personality, if available, may be useful in understanding and dealing with issues that arise in dementia. A person's premorbid low frustration tolerance, paranoia, obsessions, dependency, or poor or elevated self-esteem may surface during dementia as a reduced capacity to cope with the cognitive deficits and their social consequences (Meins, Frey and Thiesemann 1998).

## Apply appropriate practices to minimize stress

Caring for the person with dementia requires the carer to act as a surrogate for their losses.

- Memory losses in people with dementia mean carers need not only manage their life's necessities, but also tap into the remaining memory to provide mental stimulation, a sense of fulfilment and pleasure.

- Lost concept of time and place (orientation) and lost ability to process and interpret visual cues in relation to space (visuospatial losses) mean the person with dementia will get lost and will need reorientation and reassurance.

- Difficulty finding and understanding words (aphasia) and compromised working memory mean carers need to use special communication skills in communicating with the person with dementia.

- The inability to self-initiate activity means the person with dementia will need to be prompted to perform activities of daily living, and taken to the places to which they need to go.

- Loss of new thought processes will leave the person with dementia with repetitive and stereotyped thoughts, requiring the carer to express information carefully.

- Lost executive function, or an inability to problem solve or accommodate two functions at once, means tasks for the person with dementia need to be set out one at a time.

- Lost ability to filter information or focus on two things at once (attention) means care practices have to avoid distractions and create an environment free of multiple stimuli.

- The brain of a person with dementia may not process some messages relating to physiological functions such as hunger, temperature and continence, meaning others may need to predict the person's needs in these areas.

- Poor judgement that accompanies dementia means it is important to maintain a safe environment.

- Difficulty recognizing objects (agnosia) and handling objects (apraxia) means the person with dementia may need assistance with many activities such as dressing.

- Changes in muscle tone and eventual loss of motor skills require carers to compensate for those losses and provide therapy to delay them.

- Increased fatigue that accompanies dementia means carers may need to consider orchestrating frequent rests.

- A progressively reduced stress threshold means care will need to predict and manage stressors.

- Mood and behaviour changes that accompany dementia need to be accommodated with sensitive therapeutic interventions.

- Physical and mental stimulation will need to be provided to optimize function, and provide a sense of fulfilment and pleasure.

## Approach and attitude

Caring for people with dementia requires the carer to 'enter the world of the person with dementia' (Anderson, Wendler and Congdon 1998). Rather than focusing on the dementia, this involves focusing on the person as unique and equal and with a rich range of feelings and emotions (Chapman and Kerr 1996) and appreciating the *persistence of self* into advanced stages of dementia (Touhy 2004). Caring for the person with dementia involves knowing and respecting the person adult-to-adult, their family and personal values, and working as a team with the person and other carers. Carers also need to be aware that compromising behaviours arise partly as expressions of basic needs (Algase *et al.* 1996). It has been suggested that a *person-centred approach* to the care of the person with dementia will slow the effects of the dementia, and sustain functionality and quality of life (Kitwood 1997). Caregivers who strive to understand the meaning behind a person's behaviour, and who master the necessary care-giving skills and their implementation, will be more successful at curbing distressing behaviour than caregivers who act merely in a custodial role (Skovdahl, Kihlgren and Kihlgren 2003). Carers should thus see themselves as caring for a person rather than responding to a disease, and aim to:

- stimulate memory, restore self-worth

- redress or accommodate cognitive deficits

- provide stimulation and enrichment through recreational activities to mobilize the person's available cognitive resources

- prevent and defuse stress-related responses.

(American Psychiatric Association 1997)

These aims can be achieved if the following suggestions are adopted:

- Take the person with dementia seriously, identify their needs and address those needs thoughtfully. This develops trust, promotes an increased ability to function (Mintzer and Brawman-Mintzer 1996) and minimizes feelings of isolation and devaluation that can be evident in a person with dementia.

- Avoid conversations about the person with dementia within their hearing, no matter how advanced their dementia may seem. Include them in any conversation that addresses their needs, even if they are unable to contribute.

- Validate (respond to rather than correct) the personal agenda (how they try to meet a need) of the person with dementia to help restore self-worth. Others have to accept that the meaning of behaviour to a person with dementia may be different to the meaning that others may place on it. People with dementia may engage in conversation or comments based on well-ingrained memories of expressions practised throughout their life (Gwynther 1985). Although comments may be out of place in the present situation, this social facade helps them to maintain their dignity.

- Reinforce a sense of competency, without patronizing the resident or exposing failures. Search for and focus on remaining capabilities to increase self-esteem and reduce frustration.

- Use communication and care techniques which are individualized and sensitive to the person's feelings. This will be a major determinant in reducing stress-related behaviours.

- Encourage discussion of feelings of loss and loneliness where appropriate (Solomon 1993) and validate and provide encouragement.

- View agitated behaviours as a response to the person's inability to understand or cope with stress. See it as a form of self-expression that can be used to guide the responses of caregivers.

## Environment

Although the structural design of all care facilities may not be ideal for managing the needs and quality of life of people with dementia (Zeisel, Silverstein and Hyde *et al.* 2003), in many cases simple initiatives in restructuring or redecorating the care environment can help reverse the situation. People with dementia have been found to spend more time in enhanced areas featuring native or ethnic music, wall posters of nature or family scenes, and forest or citrus aromas, and in response exhibit less wandering and agitated behaviours (Burgio and Fisher 2000). Avoid stimulation that may be excessive and overburdening:

- environmental noise; telephones, machines, extractor fans

- spirited and exclusionary conversations, which can be irritating and devaluing

- television, pictures of people or mirrors if they are misinterpreted; some, however, may find family pictures or mirrors reassuring

- large groups or excessive activity

- hot or cold temperatures (Tariot 1996)

- fashion styles that are inconsistent with familiar fashions retained in the person's memory (e.g. trousers and short hair on women); these may confuse some people with dementia

- unfamiliar environments, which can be stressful for people with dementia

- well-intentioned celebrations and family outings, which can be stressful if not managed carefully so as to avoid over-stimulation

- intercoms, which can be interpreted as disembodied voices; a former railway station attendant may, however, enjoy the intercom.

Seed the environment with familiar objects, reassuring sights and cues for socially stimulating interaction, for example:

- objects from the past, old furnishings, knitting baskets and pictures reflecting past interests

- furniture arrangements conducive to social interaction; people with dementia may relate to a common area decorated like a country kitchen or old-fashioned living room

- snacks to support socially interacting groups

- high-contrast, simple memory aids, clocks, calendars, visual labels and signs to orientate or direct the person; these may need to be at wheelchair height

- reminiscent articles, such as a desk with papers for a former businessman to promote a sense of identity

- relaxing music appropriate to their era, or nature sounds

- easy access to necessary facilities such as the toilet, with colourful pictorial cues

- where possible, devices from the past that older people are more familiar with – some special purpose units have even managed to install old-fashioned fittings such as light switches as were in use many years ago

- textured materials or objects with beads and soft materials, as opposed to vinyl or plastic – older adults seem drawn to these (Hoffman 1998a).

## Communication

A reduced ability to receive and express information (language skills) in people with dementia affects the level of functioning of the individual, interferes with effective communication and can lead to social withdrawal and independently result in development of stress-related behaviour. A person's needs in communication skills should be addressed earlier in the course of dementia to help them maintain social interactions, function and quality of life (Potkins *et al.* 2003). Individuals with impaired memory are nevertheless able to transmit meaningful communication, and this communication is available to be interpreted by others. Care based on therapeutic listening techniques and interpretive communication methods may decrease the frustration created by unmet emotional and physical needs in people with dementia (Acton *et al.* 1999). Carers can use their communication skills to help make up for what the person has lost, without increasing the amount of time spent delivering care (Burgio *et al.* 2001).

It is important to adopt skills in communication.

- Seek a distraction-free environment. Consider the amount of sensory stimulation. Even music during conversation or too many people around can confuse communication efforts.

- A handshake can help the resident to focus. It will also act as a non-threatening stimulus and reinforces the carer's attentiveness.

- Use courtesy titles in addressing elderly people unless specifically requested to use a first name. Sometimes a person with dementia will relate well to a pet name such as used by a spouse, children or grandchildren.

- Determine the appropriate level of touch for each particular person. The response to extending the hand or gentle touch tells us a lot about the person and their needs. Some carers are happy to provide a cuddle. Although most people with dementia will benefit from this expression of affection, this type of physical contact should only be provided by carers who are comfortable in doing so. Gently stroking or massaging the person's hand can be a particularly worthwhile accompaniment to communication. We need to appreciate that cultural factors may determine appropriate issues of distance and physical contact. In today's legalistic environment it might be advisable for care facilities to establish protocols for the provision of physical contact by carers, and for their response to a need of the person with dementia for physical contact.

- Identify yourself, approach from the front, keep your face in the direct line of vision, gain attention, explain to the person what you are doing and what you plan to do, and ask permission.

- Use a calm, caring voice, exhibit attentiveness, and use touch where appropriate. The ability to feel and sense emotions (fear, joy, excitement, pride, anxiety, sorrow, shame, sympathy) should be assumed to remain intact in people with dementia.

- Talk slowly and use simple language. Working memory difficulties (the memory involved in holding information for the processing of present activities) can interfere with verbal comprehension. Presenting the person with complex sentences increases the demands on memory and compromises sentence comprehension because the more complex the sentence is, the longer it has to be held in working memory to be deciphered.

- Use direct statements, one-step requests, limit choices and be prepared to repeat requests. Allow some time after a verbal prompt for the information to 'sink in' (Lichtenberg and MacNeill 1998).

- Use body language, facial expression, visual demonstration and mime to emphasize what you are saying (Taylor, Ray and Meador 1995). (For example, hold up an item of clothing or mimic brushing teeth.) People with dementia may be very dependent on body language and tone of voice for communication. However, deficient visuospatial skills may cause patients to misread facial expressions (Litchenberg and MacNeill 1998).

- Avoid patronizing comments or tone of voice. Elderly people have been found to devalue the carer who maintains a patronizing speech style (Ryan, Kennaley and Pratt *et al.* 2000). The use of terms such as 'dear' or 'darling' or phrases normally reserved for a child can be patronizing. Such terms may, however, be appropriate if based on a genuine relationship.

- Explain to wheelchair patients your intention before whisking them away.

- Remember that if the person with dementia cannot see something, then as far as they are concerned, it isn't there.

- If the ability to tell the time has been lost, communicate time in relation to meals.

- Avoid unnecessary interrogation. Don't ask people who don't know where they are, where they are going.

- Involve the person with dementia in discussions in their presence to build up trust and involve them in decisions involving their care. This is especially important to build up trust in people who are suspicious. Such people may also mistrust a warm, friendly attitude but respond to a firm but kind approach (Szwabo and Boesch 1993).

- Use appropriate phraseology: Avoid 'don't' and 'no' in favour of positive suggestions and directions. Rather than 'Don't urinate in the pot plant Mr P', say 'Mr P would you like to urinate in the toilet – come and I'll show you where it is.'

- Avoid open-ended questions such as 'What would you like?', in favour of 'Would you like A or B?'. Use right-branching questions: 'Would you like to drink orange or lemon juice?' rather than 'Would you like orange or lemon juice to drink?'. Avoid unavailable choices: 'Would you like to take your medicine now?'

- Use communication aids such as message boards for people with speech difficulties but who can read. Individual books featuring pages with various prompts and responses are also useful.

- Validation therapy is a structured method of communication and can be used to redress some communication issues that arise in dementia (Feil 1998).

- If a person with dementia is non-receptive to a request, it may be better to explain that you will return to see if they are ready to respond later on.

> Mrs M, who has lost her false teeth, says 'That old bag in the corner is always stealing my teeth'.
>
> Validation involves: centring or first achieving self-control, agreeing ('Oh dear, Mrs M, you really need those teeth, don't you?'), rephrasing ('She is always stealing your teeth?'), imagining the opposite ('Is there any time she doesn't steal your teeth?') and reminiscence ('Have you often had a problem with your teeth in the past?').

An 85-year-old woman spent most of her time in bed. She used a cane on anyone who came within her reach. Staff removed the cane, which brought about furious outbursts. Medication was considered. One day it was suggested at a staff meeting that staff might need to respect this lady's bed and surrounds as the only place on earth that could be considered her territory and which she thus defended with such vigour. When staff asked permission to assist her in her daily activities the cane was no longer used. On occasions that she was agitated they explained that they would return a little later to see if she was ready.

## Care practices

Practise care from an independence-enhancing perspective rather than a dependence-supporting perspective (Rogers *et al.* 1999).

- Search for and encourage persistence with past abilities and enable as much resident independence, success and self-care as possible, while avoiding feelings of failure. For example, lay clothes out in order if this helps the person to complete dressing. Velcro fasteners may allow more involvement in dressing.

- Pictures of drawer contents on drawers, and pictures of dressing sequences may assist self-dressing. Some people with dementia may prefer the reassurance of staff contact at the expense of independence. In this case carers will need to encourage the maintenance of independence while providing emotional reassurance.

- Innovative clothing design, such as night apparel that opens at the back, facilitates care.

- Simplify tasks. Divide dressing, bathing, oral hygiene and grooming procedures into a chain of smaller, discrete tasks to accommodate deficits in working memory.

- People with dementia may be capable of some new learning (Bird 1998; Clare *et al.* 2000). It is thus feasible to intervene with everyday memory problems in the early stages of dementia and to attempt to retrain some functions.

- Some people with dementia who cannot initiate self-care may be able to imitate self-care that is demonstrated, or complete self-care that is initiated. Picture books can be used to prompt activities such as bathing.

- Encourage and practise mobility. Increasing muscular rigidity is characteristic of dementia, and people with dementia will lose the ability to walk if they remain immobilized (Dawson *et al.* 1986).

Adopt care practices that will minimize the person's stress. Aim at uniformity of care with a predictable routine of daily activity to minimize the demands on cognitive planning.

- Understand and appreciate what is normal behaviour for each individual. Accommodate idiosyncrasies.

- Adopt daily care practices and routines to simulate former habits practised at home, and recognize individual differences in preferred patterns of care (Burgener, Shimer and Murrell 1993).

- Give choices, where possible, of food, clothing and activity.

Persons with dementia living in residential care will adjust with less stress...

...if allowed to maintain their hobbies and lifestyle habits.

- While promoting independence, avoid demands that exceed cognitive capacity. Such could include 'over-encouragement' to perform tasks, answer questions or remember things. Task failure can lead to a substantial emotional reaction (Lehninger, Ravindran and Stewart 1998). Some tasks should be avoided. Put at ease residents who become frustrated when they fail to achieve a task.

- Minimize the number of caregivers providing care to the one individual. Ensure that at least one key carer gets to know about the person's family, friends and history. Confused residents may be unable to cope with too many carers or carers with whom they are not familiar.

- If the person you are trying to help is uncooperative, go away and try again later.

Provide care with respect to physical disability.

- Check for pain or tenderness and adopt care practices that avoid discomfort.

- Be aware of medical conditions that may necessitate individualized care practices.

- Predict and manage the person's physiological needs such as hunger, temperature and continence.

- Observe for and report any change in function over time during attention to activities of daily living. These could be drug side-effects or developing medical conditions, which may only be identified by someone providing day-to-day hands-on care.

- Consider hemi-attention in stroke patients. In this condition the brain may not process all that the eye sees. These people may not see what the affected side of the brain normally processes; they may eat half a meal and they may process visual clues from only one wall of a hallway.

## Activities/techniques

Offer daily activities/relationships that are meaningful and satisfying to the person with dementia. Experiment with activities that include patterns of activities they have enjoyed throughout life, and interests such as craft and dance. Activities that mimic occupational or domestic activities may be useful. For many residents in residential care facilities, it will be necessary to avoid large multi-purpose rooms where several activities are conducted concurrently, and distractions such as television.

> Mr Francis became very agitated on admission to the nursing home. For comfort he was dressed in the traditional tracksuit and sneakers. When it was discovered that he had been a senior executive in a major bank until retirement, he was dressed for the day in a suit and tie.

### OFFER PHYSICAL STIMULATION

Combining increased physical activity with improvement in the night-time nursing home environment can improve sleep and decrease agitation in nursing home residents (Alessi *et al.* 1999). Group walks, simple beach-ball games and dancing, as 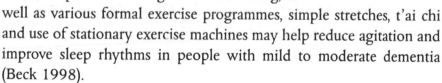 well as various formal exercise programmes, simple stretches, t'ai chi and use of stationary exercise machines may help reduce agitation and improve sleep rhythms in people with mild to moderate dementia (Beck 1998).

### OFFER MENTAL STIMULATION

Reminiscence work, possibly based on information from the family, can help carers to discover what the person with dementia can remember as opposed to what they have forgotten. This will also help the carer to understand the resident's past and communicate more effectively in the present (Gibson 1991). Reminiscence provides satisfaction and a sense of achievement and addresses the inability of the people with dementia

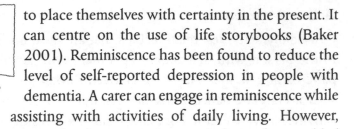

to place themselves with certainty in the present. It can centre on the use of life storybooks (Baker 2001). Reminiscence has been found to reduce the level of self-reported depression in people with dementia. A carer can engage in reminiscence while assisting with activities of daily living. However, we must also be aware that reminders of a troubled past can have unsettling results. Clues to troubling past experiences may enable the carers to target reassurance appropriately. Art, dance/ movement, literature and poetry activities may be beneficial in people with dementia (Mintzer, Hoernig and Mirski 1998). Art therapy can be used as a 'small window to the inner world' of the person with dementia when the disease process makes language and other forms of appropriate expression difficult (Gerdner 2000).

Simple mental activity such as playing bingo has been shown to have a beneficial effect on short-term memory, concentration and word retrieval in Alzheimer's patients (Sobel 2001).

Occupational therapy can be based on past work activities. The need to feel useful is a powerful force. Some menial tasks such as folding the laundry can be gratifying, and traditional domestic chores such as supervised assistance in the kitchen are often used as occupational therapy for people with dementia. Items to satisfy occupational memories, such as clipboards or safe tools, provide a connection to the past.

Encourage reading with the provision of material suitable to the individual's reading ability in terms of eyesight, cognition and subject interests. General reading skills have been found to be somewhat resistant to dementia; however, the ability to comprehend material containing unfamiliar words or concepts will be lost earlier than the comprehension of familiar words and concepts (Passafiume, Di Giacomo and Giubilei 2000).

Music therapy has proved to be a valuable tool in providing a stress-benign environment and may stimulate cognitive function (Clark, Lipe and Bilbrey 1998) and facilitate a person's adjustment to life in a long-term care facility (Kydd 2001). Musicality and singing seem to be preserved longer than language functions in people with dementia. People whose language skills have been lost may still be able to appreciate or play music and sing beautifully. Naturally music from days gone by and by familiar artists of their younger days will be better appreciated by the older person with dementia. Live music may be more effective in increasing levels of engagement and well-being (Sherratt, Thornton and Hatton 2004).

- Montessori-based activity programming has been claimed to benefit people with dementia (Orsulic-Jeras, Judge and Camp 2000). This is a programme initially developed to teach children. It uses activities or 'lessons' based on principles used in occupational therapy. It may involve breaking down tasks into steps and programming activities to progress from simple to complex and from concrete to abstract. Activities may involve sorting pictures into categories or memory games.

- Trivia, reading or discussion groups are common formats for providing mental stimulation in residential care facilities, but groups need to be small in the case of individuals with cognitive losses.

- 'Busy boxes' containing fabrics, keys, stuffed animals, pegs, fabric-covered books and general household paraphernalia may provide stimulation, distraction or comfort (Mayers and Griffin 1990). People with dementia seem to enjoy seeing and touching soft colours and textures, which could be cut out of remnants (Hall *et al.* 1986). (Care needs to be taken with smaller objects which may find their way into the mouths of people with dementia.)

- Sensory training has been observed to produce gains in orientation, tension, concentration, self-feeding, mobility, communication and the ability to cooperate with care giving. Sensory training involves formal sessions where residents are exposed to various sensory stimuli (Malone 1996).

- The implementation of the Eden Alternative model has been credited with lower levels of distress in terms of boredom and helplessness of residents of a long-term care facility (Bergman-Evans 2004). The Eden Alternative addresses the need for companionship, the need to nurture other living things and the need for variety and spontaneity in one's daily life. It suggests a programme involving animals, the daily infusion of children into the life of residential care residents, the profusion of plants and gardens, the transformation of facility management style and involvement of the local community. The provision of gardens in raised troughs will assist and encourage gardening by people with dementia and physical disability.

- Memory books contain images and brief simple sentences that use the preserved abilities of people with dementia to improve the structure and quality of communication and reduce ambiguity (Bourgeois 1990) and hence frustration.

- There is some evidence that reality orientation has benefits on both cognition and behaviour for people with dementia (Spetor *et al.* 2000) but it may require a continued programme to sustain potential benefits, and in some people may only increase frustration.

PROVIDE REST AND RELAXATION

- Minimize fatigue with rest breaks or quiet times, especially after activity. Regular physical exercise, however, decreases overall fatigue and helps to ensure a diurnal rhythm, and should be maintained (Hall 1994). Activity times should be reduced as the disease progresses. Place chairs as environmental cues to rest.

- Pleasant smells can reduce stress. Studies have reported beneficial effects from aromatherapy on agitation, and improved quality of life (Burns, Ballard and Holmes 2002; Holmes, Hopkins and Hensford *et al.* 2002). Smell impulses are, in fact, claimed to travel a faster route to the emotional centre of the brain than other stimuli (Brawley 1998).

- Gentle massage techniques, even if concentrating on the hands or shoulders, can satisfy a longing for touch that may be evident in many elderly people (Connelly 1999). Having the hair brushed can be particularly relaxing for some people.

3

# Addressing stress-related responses

## Hostile verbal and physical responses

People with dementia whose stress threshold has been exceeded may respond by hitting, kicking, scratching, abusing, cursing, biting or spitting.

*Defusing an acute verbal or physical episode*

- Allow the most effective staff members to take the lead (Wick and Reid 1997).

- Introduce yourself appropriately, position yourself at the person's level, be calm, speak softly, use eye contact, ask permission, and explain what needs to happen.

- Isolate the person and divert attention from the event.

- Distract or redirect the person, using their lack of short-term memory to advantage.

- Investigate fears; validate the person's concerns.

- Use a gentle touch (e.g. hold hands) where appropriate.

- Give choices and offer reassurance.

- Minimize environmental stimuli.

- Place something in the person's hands to avoid use of their hands to resist essential care.

- Keep dangerous objects out of reach.

## Assessment of verbal or physical responses

Assessment tools are useful to gain a fuller and more accurate under-standing of a given behaviour. They might be used as a guide towards effective care strategies, and as a benchmark against which to measure progress (Cohen-Mansfield 1999). The ABC approach looks at the questions to ask when confronted with these behaviours.

*Antecedents* – Ask about and search for stressors that might have provoked the behaviour.

*Behaviour* – Document all aspects of the behaviour. What is happening, where, when, how often?

*Consequences* – Note the consequences of the behaviour for the person concerned and others.

Check that expectations of the behaviour are realistic and consider if the behaviour is harming anyone or affecting the patients' well-being. Avoid misinterpreting or overreacting to the incident. A 'grasp reflex', evident in late dementia, in which the person may be unable to release their grip voluntarily, may be misinterpreted as an attempt to resist or hurt a carer. Resistance to the appropriate positioning of limbs for dressing can be an involuntary resistance to passive movement (sometimes called the Gegenhalten response). Consider if the person is directing anger towards a carer or is simply trying to remove an unpleasant stimulus. Case conferences are an important initiative in optimizing care of people with dementia. Certain carers will often have developed specific care practices that should be shared with all carers. Whereas in many cases one carer will report a particular concern in relation to a resident's behaviour, another carer will report that their style of approach results in no similar concerns. Case conferences will provide an opportunity for care personnel to share their successful strategies, encourage and facilitate the care staff who do experience difficulties and promote a uniform understanding of the person and a more consistent approach to interaction and care. In one model of care, a group process to educate carers and manage behaviour involves the respective resident in the discussion, or involves all the residents in group discussions (Swift, Williams and Potter 2002).

## *Preventing hostile verbal or physical responses*
### IDENTIFY CAUSE/MEANING OF STRESS

Understanding the behaviour is the first step. Behaviours may have a special meaning to the elderly individual with dementia, which might differ from the meaning inferred by the observer. Seemingly dysfunctional acts may be the person's only communication tool available at a time of stress or fear. Passive resistance to care may be inappropriately documented as aggression. Only two per cent of aggressive events have been found to occur without an antecedent (Katz 2000). In over 70 per cent of cases staff contact has represented the immediate precipitant of an aggressive event (Ryden, Bossenmaier and McLauchlan 1991). Thus staff care techniques will be an important element in limiting verbally or physically aggressive resistance to care. Caregivers who are more accepting of the care-giving situation and are more sensitive to dementia-related problems are claimed to report less hyperactivity symptoms in those for whom they care than caregivers who are less sensitive to their care situation (de Vugt *et al.* 2004).

In over 70% of cases staff contact has represented the immediate precipitant of an agressive event

Ask questions and refer to experienced personnel or the case conference to search for and identify the stresses that may be precipitating agitated behaviours. Besides talking with the person, source visitors and relatives as appropriate, as well as carers including domestic care staff, for clues as to what could precipitate agitated behaviours. Triggers may involve any necessary activity in the daily care routine and will provide clues to successful care techniques. Refer any emerging medical condition for assessment.

REDRESS STRESSORS

Examples of stressors that can lead to aggressive verbal or physical responses include:

- a perception that personal space has been invaded

- pain or anticipation of pain

- depression; people with dementia who manifested physical or verbal aggression have been found to have a higher prevalence of depression than those without such behaviours (Menon *et al.* 2001); specifically, screaming may be associated with depression (Cohen-Mansfield, Werner and Marx 1990)

- medical conditions such as constipation, vaginitis, or urinary tract infection (see under pp.17–19)

- elimination needs or an incontinent episode (the person may have been punished for being wet as a child)

- frustration at the inability to communicate

- frustration at forgetfulness

- confrontation with reality, and finding the present situation unacceptable

- inability to complete a task

- being scolded

- misinterpretation of situation owing, for example, to poor eyesight or hearing, or being suddenly awakened

- misidentification of a carer

- distressing or unpleasant interactions with other residents

- delusional misidentification, hallucinations or illusions (misinterpreted shadows) (Hwang *et al.* 1999)

- music, TV, radio programme or particular chores

- changes in the sequence of daily activities, environment or carer (Banazak 1996)

- loneliness, lack of personal contact, boredom, grief or fear

- heat, cold, noise, the need to go to the toilet or hunger

- drug toxicity or delirium

- memory of childhood events or unresolved inner conflicts; sometimes this information will not be offered, and may be inappropriate to investigate or may only be offered in the sanctity of the medical practitioner's office

- unmet needs in relation to cultural, social, spiritual, domestic, environmental and occupational history or prior lifestyle

- restraints; policies for the use of restraints are well documented and reductions in the use of restraints and reliance on restraint alternatives have been found to be possible without an increase in serious injuries (Neufeld, Libow and Foley *et al.* 1999).

Examples of responses to these stressors include:

- feelings of shame or inadequacy at, for example, failing to complete a task

- actions that could normally be controlled becoming disinhibited; alternatively, damaged brain processes may result in aggressive behaviours (Holden and Chapman 1994)

- simply wanting to be left alone; attention to care, although necessary, is against the person with dementia's will

- agitated behaviours; these may be a response to pain in people who are unable to articulate that they feel pain. To examine pain in cognitively impaired adults, ask simple yes/no questions and look for non-verbal cues such as vocalizations, crying out, wincing, wrinkling of forehead (especially in response to movement), restlessness, rocking, rubbing or guarding the affected area, resistance to personal care that requires movement (Feldt, Warne and Ryden 1998). Investigate for unreported fractures. A trial of paracetamol given regularly in association with a pain chart may be an appropriate means by which to investigate pain.

Sensitive application of care principles for people with dementia and the removing of stressors as described above may reduce aggressive episodes. In many cases this will simply involve reassurance, and the type of reassurance will need to be incorporated into daily care to prevent reemergence of the stress, for example:

- remove any offending stimuli

- treat pain

- address unmet needs

- validate and reassuringly address issues from past traumatic events

- medical issues will require referral for treatment

- check appropriate approach and communication techniques

- be prepared to defer care.

## General management issues for agitated behaviours

Try to recognize and document warning signs in those people who are prone to verbal or physical reactions. Look for changes in physical activity (fidgeting, repetitive actions, pacing, changed expression, moving things), verbal activity or mood. Target appropriate interventions early.

Use trial and error to discover general approaches, environmental modification, communication techniques and activities that may reduce stress (see pp.24–31). Monitor the presentation of any medical problems and seek appropriate treatment. Reinforcement of positive behaviour is strongly recommended in the literature for stress-related behaviours (Landreville *et al.* 1998).

Various 'disciplinary-type' approaches such as reinforcement of the need to comply with appropriate standards, recognizing appropriate behaviour, restriction, denying favourite activities, time out, and removal to an area where positive reinforcement is not possible have been used to address aggressive behaviours (Cohen-Mansfield 1989). Such techniques would only be appropriate in selected people and where the behaviour is not in response to a reversible stress.

Aim to use care-based therapy, rather than drug therapy, so long as there are no overt psychotic symptoms (Mansdorf *et al.* 1999). Short-term medication therapy may be appropriate to ameliorate agitation while non-drug interventions are explored. Short courses of medication therapy may be appropriate and useful in the management of verbal or physical reactions if early warning signs can be identified. Care staff will often be responsible for ensuring the appropriate use and termination of any such therapy.

## *Bathing strategies*

People with dementia may not associate bathing with the purpose of bathing or even understand the sensation of water. Bathing is a common precipitant of stress. Many of this generation did not bathe daily, or may have bathed in the evening, and they may not see any reason why this should change. Many will consider the event an uninvited invasion of privacy. Bathing should be attended to as a therapeutic intervention rather than a task (the car-wash approach) (Hoeffer *et al.* 1997).

- Try as much as possible to use the same carer to assist with bathing and respect the gender preferences of the resident.

- Use appropriate techniques referred to in Chapter 2, pp.22–34:

- approach (take seriously, validate, reinforce a sense of competency)

- environment (music or aromatherapy are just as important in bathrooms)

- communication (identify yourself, ask permission, explain)

- care (check for pain or tenderness, give choices, simplify tasks).

- Individualize procedures as much as possible, attempting to recreate the person's life-long bathing practice. Offer bathing at a different time in the day if necessary.

- Check that the experience does not produce discomfort. Confirm that the water temperature is suitable for that person. It may be necessary to administer two paracetamol tablets an hour prior to care procedures for people for whom such procedures are accompanied by pain despite the most careful technique.

- Incorporate pleasurable activities such as 'small talk' and reminiscence.

- Let the person hear and feel the sound of running water first. Wash feet then work upwards.

- Some residents may prefer to use a bath. This raises obvious problems. However, we should consider that some residents might have no historic experience of, or may have adverse recollections of, water spraying on them. In this case the person may be sponged using minimal water flow from a tap or shower.

- Allow the person use of a washcloth: no matter how inefficiently it may be used, it may provide a sense of independence and reduce frustration.

- Allow a modesty garment to be worn while bathing. This can simply be a swimming costume or trunks, undergarments, or a light open-backed gown allowing washing access underneath (Namazi and Johnson 1996).

At changeover, the carers are complaining about how aggressive Mrs J is when being showered. A junior carer pipes up, 'I don't have any trouble. I ask her to turn on the water, which I adjust, and give her the soap, while I use another cake.'

- Bathe residents who find bathing stressful no more often than necessary for hygiene.

- Separate shampooing hair, which can be frightening, from the bathing activity.

- It may be necessary to offer to defer bathing.

- Utilize bed baths where traditional bathing is unacceptable.

- Administrative procedures should support the alteration of standard routines by carers, in seeking appropriate, individualized, resident-focused care techniques.

- Record, document and communicate successful interventions.

Mr MacDonald, who is normally a placid man, becomes very agitated and resistive when showered. Investigation of his past activities finds that he was a farmer who looked after sheep. This involved putting sheep into an enclosed pen where chemical was sprayed on them to eradicate lice and blowfly larvae. Mr MacDonald was happy to be sat in the shower cubicle and sponged from a bucket of warm water.

## Toileting strategies

Toileting can be a problem for people with dementia; because they do not recognize the need to use the toilet, or because they find the care involved in the toileting procedure stressful (Hutchinson, Leger-Krall and Wilson 1996), or because of the effects of constipation, incontinence or painful toileting. Constipation can result in increased confusion and stress-related behaviours in people with dementia.

People with dementia may no longer feel sensations from the involuntary anal sphincter that tell them that they need to go to the toilet. Failure to recognize stimulus from the voluntary sphincter will result in incontinence or inappropriate withholding of faeces. Some may recognize the urges but not associate them correctly, or be apprehensive of toileting due to discomfort or the anticipated care procedure. Others may not identify the present toileting facilities with their purpose. Some have practised toileting techniques considered curious by usual standards.

Whether the toileting event is complicated or stressful, people with dementia will benefit from bowel hygiene measures that avoid constipation and thus facilitate appropriate toileting.

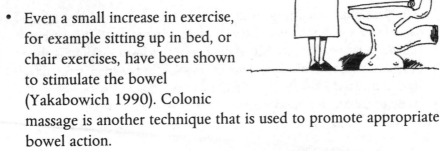

- Utilize an individualized bowel protocol including fluid, fibre, plentiful fresh fruit and exercise as appropriate, with faecal softeners added, if necessary, to prevent constipation.

- Even a small increase in exercise, for example sitting up in bed, or chair exercises, have been shown to stimulate the bowel (Yakabowich 1990). Colonic massage is another technique that is used to promote appropriate bowel action.

- Be vigilant for cues that indicate a need to use the toilet. Such cues could be fidgeting, holding back, walking around or irritability.

- Ensure the person is comfortable and allow plenty of time to use the toilet.

- Try to identify a pattern to toileting activity. This may involve regular toileting to identify a pattern.

APPROACHES FOR PEOPLE WHO RESIST TOILETING

- Use appropriate techniques referred to in Chapter 2 (pp.22–34):
  - approach (take seriously, validate, reinforce a sense of competency)
  - environment (free of distraction, relaxing music, aromatherapy)
  - communication (identify yourself, ask permission, explain)
  - care (give choices, simplify tasks).

- Try as much as possible to use the same carer to assist with toileting and respect the gender preferences of the resident.

- Identify and address causes of pain or discomfort such as from haemorrhoids.

- Incorporate pleasurable activities, 'small talk' and reminiscence while providing appropriate assistance.

- Allow as much privacy as practicable. It may be necessary to wait outside the closed door until assistance is necessary.

- Individualize procedures with respect to patient preferences.

In late dementia, patients may handle faecal matter because they have lost the usual revulsion felt towards faeces. Achieving appropriate evacuation of faeces by the above practices may be the best means of avoiding problems.

## Verbally agitated behaviours

Non-aggressive verbal agitation can present as screaming, repetitive, purposeless vocalizations or repeated requests for help. These are often of particular concern in residential care facilities because the calling may be disruptive to other residents and it is often difficult to explain or resolve the behaviour. Verbal behaviours may or may not be a response to stress. In early dementia, people may be noisy due to boredom or lack of stimulation, or they may be seeking attention or find the repeated verbal activity comforting. These people invariably respond to attention when available. Others may call out because of stress or frustration. In others we use the term 'cerebral irritation' as if there is some lesion in the brain disrupting control pathways. Some people say they know they are calling out but are unable to stop it. In late dementia calling out could be due to a delusion or hallucination. Addressing verbal behaviours may involve patiently experimenting with a range of interventions designed to remove or distract from the cause.

### *Approaches to investigating and dealing with verbal agitation*

- Determine if the verbal behaviour represents distress to the person or significant disruption to the lives of others.

- Ask the person why they are calling out.

- Investigate needs. The calling-out may be a frustrated attempt to communicate unmet needs to caregivers (Allen-Burge, Stevens and Burgio 1999). Investigate hunger or thirst and offer food or drink (Beck and Vogelpohl 1999).

- Provide appropriate reassurance and care approaches; calling out could be in anticipation of the discomfort of care procedures.

- Assess for pain, infection, constipation or other medical conditions. A trial of paracetamol given regularly may be an appropriate means by which to investigate pain. Investigate for unreported fractures. People exhibiting disruptive vocalizations have been found to receive significantly less analgesic

medication than non-disruptive individuals (Kaasalainen *et al.* 1998).

- Allow structured rest periods; people exhibiting verbal agitation may be fatigued.

- See if spending a little time with the person helps, simply by paying them attention and responding to their needs.

- Repositioning or *gentle* massage may defuse verbal agitation.

- Consider smell, noise, light, activity and temperature; these can prompt agitated behaviours (Coulson 2000) and may need to be addressed.

- On the other hand, it may be worth trialling increased activity or social stimulation. Even bed-bound patients may respond to exposure to an active environment.

- Address hearing and vision deficits. Wax build-up in the cars is a common cause of hearing deficit. Hearing aids may have flat batteries.

- Provide auditory stimuli such as music, possibly via headphones in some cases.

- Provide white noise such as ocean sounds, nature sounds such as bird calls, or heartbeat rhythms as experienced in the

NATURE SOUNDS CAN BE USED TO REDUCE AGITATION

womb. Recordings of such sounds can be purchased (or made), and bedside devices that play a variety of white noise sounds are available in retail stores. Residents exhibiting screaming behaviours have been observed to settle under a hair dryer (Burgio *et al.* 1996).

- Audiotapes or videotapes of a family member (Doyle *et al.* 1997) recounting cherished memories, possibly incorporating pauses for responses and music, may provide appropriate stimulation.

- Audio amplification devices have been utilized to enable residents with a hearing deficit to experience that their vocalizations are audible (Cariaga *et al.* 1991).

- A vibrating or rocking bed or chair may have a calming effect (Sloane *et al.* 1999).

- Experiment with olfactory stimulation (aromatherapy) or objects to touch or handle such as textured objects, household paraphernalia or harmony balls.

- People with verbally disruptive behaviours who have a predominantly depressive and labile effect warrant a trial of antidepressant therapy (Meares and Draper 1999).

- Appropriate medication therapy may be considered for people with paranoid or delusional ideation. Such conditions could be associated with verbal agitation (Eustace *et al.* 2001).

- The person may respond to being given something to suck, but if this works check for thirst or hunger.

- A psychologist may need to prescribe a procedure for reassuring a person who has been exposed to emotional trauma; such an experience in the past or inner conflicts can be positively related to the amount of screaming manifested in the present (Cohen-Mansfield *et al.* 1996).

- Reinforce quiet periods with carer attention, ceasing if verbal behaviour reoccurs. Observation of or attention to people exhibiting verbal agitation should be conducted at regular intervals distributed evenly throughout waking hours so that it is anticipated (Cohen-Mansfield *et al.* 1996).

- It is also conceivable that a brain lesion could disinhibit verbal control pathways (cerebral irritation) leading to calling behaviours. Such people may have suffered a stroke and maintained normal cognitive abilities, but be unable to explain why they are calling out, and may find this distressing. A titrated trial of anticonvulsant therapy may be appropriate in this setting.

- It may be necessary to negotiate a level of care and attention for those people presenting constant inappropriate demands who are cognitively intact.

- When the usually noisy person is quiet, they may be sick.

---

Mrs P was on medication to prevent her incessant and unintelligible calling-out. A visiting consultant offered his hand while consulting with Mrs P. Mrs P turned the hand over, held it so firmly that assistance was later necessary to unclasp the hand, and proceeded to run her fingers over the captured palm and mutter. It was evident that Mrs P had a lifetime practice of palm reading and other similar practices. The provision of cards, palm drawings and associated paraphernalia enabled Mrs P to be drug free. Interestingly Mrs P's husband had not seen fit to provide this information.

---

## Wandering

Interventions to address wandering are only necessary if the wandering presents safety issues or represents distress. An acute phase of wandering should prompt medical investigation for an acute event or stressor such as a urinary tract infection or constipation. Chronic wandering is more likely to be a result of the process of dementia but could also be due to a reversible medical condition.

Wandering in a person with dementia can be:

- a means of coping with stress

- a continuation of lifestyle patterns

- the person seeking to make sense of the environment

- the person seeking security in familiar faces, something recognizable or a dead spouse

- the person seeking to abscond from an unpleasant environment, or wanting to go home; requests to go 'home' will usually mean the childhood home, but the word 'home' can represent a time when life was more comfortable

- faulty goal-directed behaviour with something in mind that the person wants to do

- the act of following people around, possibly for reassurance

- the person seeing the exit sign or seeing others leaving

- a response to boredom and a need for stimulation

- a purposeful but dangerous adventure to access shopping needs

- a functional response, which relieves anxiety and tension in individuals who were traditionally action-orientated (Rapp *et al.* 1992); high levels of past social and leisure activities have been associated with wandering (Hall 1994)

- the person attempting to escape some distressing event, or routine emerging from long-term or childhood memory

- a result of neurological damage (cerebral irritation).

Acute presentations of wandering may be due to:

- thirst, pain, discomfort or the need to toilet

- depression, delusions, hallucinations or anxiety

- hypoxia (lack of oxygen), which could be due to a lung or heart condition or anaemia, and may manifest in restlessness and pacing (Matteson, Linton and Linton 1996)

- akathisia – a condition often induced by antipsychotic medication, characterized by involuntary movements which can present as 'ants in the pants'-type fidgeting. It can also present as irrepressible pacing. Akathisia can also be misinterpreted as a worsening of behavioural symptoms

- the emergence of practically any medical burden.

Agitation and wandering late in the day ('sundowning') may be due to:

- a daily cycle of delirium; it could be that changes in physiological or psychological function during the course of each day could eventuate in increased confusion leading to agitated behaviours. Fatigue or dehydration, for example, could develop during the course of each day. Disturbances of the daily cycle of body temperature change caused by Alzheimer's disease have been proposed as a cause of sundowning (Volicer *et al.* 2001)

- a change of shift in the care facility, which represents a sudden change in the facility environment (Bliwise 2000)

- the person feeling the need to search for the usual family gathering at the end of the working day, or seeking normal changes that occur when returning from work.

Where wandering exposes a person with dementia to danger, interventions initially targeting identifiable causes should be trialled.

- Monitor environmental changes or activity occurring before wandering episodes to identify possible stimuli (Algase 1993).

- Assess for and address all potential reversible conditions such as pain, incontinence, infection, thirst, depression, delirium or akathisia, which may underlie wandering behaviours.

- Keep people active and engaged and enjoying themselves for as long as possible (Allan 1994) but with structured rest periods. Daily social gatherings possibly involving physical exercise may help to reduce wandering.

- Provide meaningful tasks to create a sense of usefulness and provide exercise and companionship, especially targeting sundowning. Group sessions, usually held in the afternoon, involving activities such as music, exercise, dancing or ball games, may provide a distraction from wandering or agitation.

- Alternatively, soft music played during a quiet time may help to calm people who tend to sundown.

- It has been claimed that wandering residents of residential care facilities will stay in an activity room when it looks like a place they recognize (Simard 1999). Provide visual, auditory and olfactory stimuli to simulate a home or natural outdoor environment. Provide a common area with traditional furniture and ornaments (country kitchen or cottage look) featuring music and nature or family scenes.

- Pictures and symbols can help with locating bathrooms or bedrooms.

- Trial a rest period into the afternoon schedule, or alternatively an activity session followed by a rest period.

- Provide chairs at strategic locations to cue rest.

- Search family, social and occupational history for distressing events, or clues to satisfying the resident's needs. The answer could be a reassuring statement or the provision of an activity such as a simple cleaning duty to satisfy needs.

- Address environmental risks that may be encountered by the wandering resident and provide circumscribed areas for wandering.

- Apply grids of masking tape to the floor in front of the exit door (Cohen-Mansfield 1989), place a mirror in the front of the exit door or hide the doorknob or lock with a cloth panel (Roberts 1999).

> Mr J created problems by continually wandering into the parking lot. Supervising him was a nightmare and restraint was considered. An assessment of his customary habits revealed that he had been a car salesman. Pictures of the kind of car he used to sell were put up around his room. This provided a relationship to a meaningful past.

A former businessman becomes agitated at 4 p.m. every day because in his mind it is time to go home. He is given a briefcase, says goodbye and waits (for his bus) on the seat out front. A little later staff tell him the bus is late and he is redirected back inside for a rest before dinner. His mind will have moved on from 'going home'.

- Fit personal alarm devices.

- Organize group walks or drives for wanderers.

- Bright light therapy such as 30 minutes' daily exposure to 10,000-lux bright light has been claimed to have a positive effect on motor restless behaviour (Haffmans *et al.* 2001).

- Manage change of shift so as not to disorientate residents. This could involve conducting activities during the change of shift or staggering shift changes.

- Showing a night wanderer that it is dark outside may orientate them to the fact that it is a time for sleep.

Mrs C had the habit of negotiating a dangerous, busy street to buy cigarettes. Buying Mrs C's brand of cigarettes and keeping them in the small facility shop saved her being exposed to danger.

Mrs H began her wandering, agitated behaviour most evenings. A family history was sourced. It was revealed that when she was little her alcoholic father would come home in the evening and beat her, until she eventually found a hiding place that he did not know about. She called it her 'safe place'. Staff learnt to settle her by taking her by the elbow and saying to her, 'Come on, Mrs H, I will take you to your safe place.'

## Intrusiveness, rummaging or picking behaviour

People with dementia may intrude into others' private spaces, and 'rummage' when they are lost or searching for purposeful activity. Picking behaviour is defined as rearranging, carrying about, tearing and rolling things (Johansson, Zingmark and Norberg 1999). It may represent meaningful fragments of common activities in the person's past, such as tidying up or tending to flowers. These behaviours can present a problem when they involve other people's property. People with fronto-temporal forms of dementia such as Pick's disease may constantly rearrange objects, and even put things in their mouth.

Interventions that may address these behaviours include the following:

- Provide a rummaging box or drawer full of familiar items.

- Provide objects that may connect the person with their past work or pleasure activities, or activities replicating them.

- Provide distraction, or involve the person in group activity.

- Ensure the person's room is well identified with something personal and distinct.

- Many interventions that are appropriate for verbal or wandering behaviours may be of benefit for settling intrusive behaviour.

4

# Managing feeding problems

Weight loss in dementia, particularly in those with Alzheimer's disease, is common and can be due to metabolic problems associated with the condition rather than poor appetite or food consumption. In any case enhancing eating performance will help maintain weight. Feeding difficulties can be major care issues in the later stages of dementia. Food refusal is usually more common as the condition progresses (Draper, Brodaty and Low 2002). The evaluation of nutritional status and management of eating behaviour can be important considerations in the care of people with dementia (Brocker *et al.* 2003). An eating 'diary' should be a first step to determine the actual amount of food being consumed. Factors contributing to poor eating performance include:

- cognitive loss
- swallowing difficulty (dysphagia)
- distractions
- agitation and restlessness
- poor hand-to-mouth coordination
- oral problems
- reduced or distorted taste sensations
- reduced sense of smell
- drug effects including nausea
- discomfort, pain or medical illness

- delusions about eating
- depression.

## Interventions to improve feeding

- Conduct mealtimes as a care-centred event rather than a task-orientated event.
Interactions designed to impact on physiological and social needs at mealtimes can help people with dementia to sit at the table longer and eat more food (Beattie, Algase and Song 2004).

- Apply appropriate approach, environment, communication and care practices to minimize stress (see Chapter 2 pp.22–34).

- When assisting feeding sit face to face with the person, socially engaging the person in the process. The person with dementia may interpret feeding from behind or beside, especially in the absence of social engagement, as a dismembered spoon miraculously appearing out of nowhere and seeking out the mouth.

- Ask the person why they are eating poorly or not eating normally.

- Involve close family members in seeking information relating to preferred eating habits.

- Assess for medical conditions such as nausea or constipation and psychiatric disorders.

- Instigate a medication review, specifically for advice on drugs that may affect taste or cause nausea or gastrointestinal distress.

- Activity prior to a meal may need to be stress-free and quiet.

- Avoid unnecessary background noises and distractions, such as TV.

- Low light, nature sounds and music have been proposed as interventions to increase food consumption and reduce the length of feeding time (Beck and Shue 1994).

- Utilize small groups of compatible residents around a table.

- Sit functionally impaired people opposite people who have retained the ability to feed themselves; this may help by allowing them to mimic the feeding process (Allen-Burge et al. 1999).

- Match the person's past environment; eating habits may become more functional in a more formal eating setting.

- Elderly people may have changes in visual, taste and smell (olfactory) sensations. Appetizing aromas and stimulating food tastes may address this. Experiment with the use of spices and flavours to address any loss of taste sensations. Specialized dementia units, which provide visual access to the kitchen, have claimed significant improvements in residents' social behaviour and confusion scores over time (Archibald 1994). The limitations of this intervention are obvious, but enabling appetizing smells to permeate outside the kitchen may be feasible. Brew coffee, simmer appetizing food or bake bread in a breadmaker in the dining area (Algase 1993).

- Some residents may increase food intake if provided with a bag of finger foods (Hall and Buckwalter 1991). The provision of regular finger snacks may be more cost-effective than supplements (Barratt 1999). Snacks can have the added advantage of providing activity or stimulation for people presenting stress-related behaviours associated with dementia. Mashed potato provides good glue for people who have difficulty handling sandwiches. Treats such as hot potato chips will often be accepted by someone who has ceased to persevere with a regular meal.

- Provide foods that residents remember from childhood (Hoffman 1998b).

- Provide one course at a time. Do not overfill the plate.

- Food should be of appropriate consistency but various textures should be used. With assisted feeding, offer bite-sized pieces of food, one at a time.

- People who traditionally said a blessing before dinner may need to continue that practice.

- Ensure there are visual contrasts between cutlery, foodstuffs, plate and table, because people with dementia often lose the ability to differentiate similar colours (Beck 1998). Avoid patterned placemats, plates and tablecloths. Use plates with contrasting colours to the tablecloth. Avoid serving dark food on a dark plate.

- Assignment of a specific caregiver allows that caregiver to become more aware of subtle feeding cues so that they can impute meaning to those cues.

- Avoid robbing people of their retained abilities in feeding by tailoring assistance specifically to compensate only for deficiencies. Some patients may only need food cut. Others may need it cut and placed on a utensil. Feeding skills are part of long-term memory and can be reactivated (Dawson et al. 1986). It could be that former care practices provided unnecessary assistance for reasons of expediency, resulting in deficiencies in feeding that can be reversed.

- People with dementia may view the provision of a meal as an act of charity or goodwill, or they may associate it with past experience where having a meal provided in this type of situation would incur an expense. There may also be an inability to associate food with its purpose (McGillivray and Marland 1999). Consequently it may be necessary to provide reassurance that the meal does not cost anything, and even to explain the process of eating and the purpose of food.

- Food intake is often better earlier in the day when cognitive abilities are better. Conversely, serving the main meal at night follows the more traditional eating pattern.

- Nutritional supplements may need to be planned to increase caloric intake, but should not be given at mealtimes.

- Disruptive residents may need to take meals in smaller groups and at a different time.

- For people in late-stage dementia an upward stroke of the larynx to produce a swallow reflex may be necessary.

5

# Managing inappropriate sexual activity

Inappropriate sexual behaviour can involve:

- solitary sexual acting-out, such as public masturbation or exposing body parts

- sexual acting-out involving others, such as fondling or groping carers

- engaging in sexual activity with other people in public

- inappropriate sexual talk or obscene gestures

- false sexual allegations.

People with dementia may have physical alterations in the brain structure that interfere with memory, judgement and impulse control. A genteel person with dementia may use profanely inappropriate languaage for the first time, merely because they have heard it and remember it being used. Similarly, a person with dementia who has always acted with sexual appropriateness may lose the context of appropriateness.

What is in fact appropriate or inappropriate needs to be determined by the environment of care, but with respect for the person's needs and rights. Although allowing the appropriate expression of sexuality is a duty of care, such expression in residential care may cause jealousy in some residents and precipitate inappropriate sexual behaviours in others (Haddad and Benbow 1993).

Determine and address antecedents or precipitants of inappropriate sexual behaviour.

- Ensure the availability of sufficient emotional stimulation.

- Avoid exposure to sexually explicit media or carers' comments or actions that could be misinterpreted.

- Check for delusions or mood disorder.

- Check for prescribed medications such as levodopa that may affect sexual behaviour. Sedatives or sleeping pills may disinhibit behaviour.

- Adopt care practices that minimize physical, environmental or emotional stress. Any stress that can precipitate agitation or aggression could also precipitate sexually inappropriate behaviour. Death anxiety can underlie preoccupations with sex (Philo, Richie and Kaas 1996).

- Take into account any information that has been provided about past inappropriate sexual behaviour or exposure to sexual abuse in the past.

- Avoid being judgemental. Avoid overreaction or confrontation. Respond calmly and firmly, while distracting, redirecting and refocusing the person (Wlosinski and Diaello 2001). Reinforce appropriate behaviour.

- If the activity is only inappropriate due to public exposure, redirect to a private environment. Explain gently why the behaviour is inappropriate. Explain the situation tactfully to witnesses of the behaviour with assurances such as 'Mr Smith forgot that there were other people out here.'

- Inappropriate sexual behaviour can be due to social isolation or a need for intimacy, attention or affection, and may be able to be modified with an increased level of appropriate affection or contact (Buckwalter 1995), such as touch, hand or back massage or the offer of soothing activity or objects. Naturally, avoid any such physical intervention if counterproductive.

- Place objects in the hands of people who 'grope' carers when attending to activities of daily living.

- Check whether people who disrobe or expose themselves are too hot, uncomfortable, have a lack of clothing support (belt, braces), have a need to void, or suffer genital irritation due to a skin condition or faecal impaction.

- It might be appropriate to encourage professional discussion of issues relating to sexual behaviour and sexual frustration.

- In some cases counselling or a gentle disciplinary approach may be necessary.

- If inappropriate behaviour is not amenable to behavioural redirection and if underlying causes have been addressed, refer for medical assessment. In some cases medication therapy is beneficial, safe and appropriate.

- Some difficult situations, such as a married person connecting with another resident in residential care facility in a manner that presents concern to a spouse, may necessitate consultation between concerned parties, facility management and a professional consultant or counsellor.

- Avoid taking sexual insults from a person with dementia personally. Avoid being judgemental about sexually inappropriate behaviours and demonstrating disgust at such behaviours.

# 6

# Managing sleep disturbance

## Factors affecting sleep in elderly people with dementia

The segregation of sleep into dark and light cycles breaks down with age, resulting in decreased nocturnal sleep and the tendency to nap in the daytime. There is a substantial reduction in the amount of deep sleep, and an increase in light or rapid-eye-movement sleep. An elderly person may have an inappropriate expectation of sleep. Lonely or depressed people may embrace sleep to fill empty hours, and residential care can lead to long periods in bed. Depression and cognitive disorders contribute further to a disrupted sleep–wake cycle. In addition people with Alzheimer's dementia may have altered circadian rhythms of sleep, manifesting in multiple periods of sleep and waking, daytime naps and sundowning as well as a higher prevalence of sleep apnoea (Reynolds *et al.* 1988). These people cannot conform to regimented sleep routines. None of these situations are indications for drug therapy. In many cases claims of insufficient sleep are not valid. After daytime naps and early retiring, many elderly people may have achieved their necessary six hours' daily sleep well before the normal rising time.

## Interventions to improve sleep

- Utilize a sleep diary to document sleep patterns. In many cases this may actually indicate that sleep is adequate (Mant and Bearpark 1990; Bachman 1992).

- Address underlying causes of insomnia such as pain (which is often unreported), depression that can disrupt the sleep–wake cycle (Folks and Burke 1998), psychosis, sleep apnoea, Parkinson's disease, heart failure, asthma, gastro-oesophageal reflux or restless leg syndrome.

- Avoid giving caffeine (coffee, tea, cola, chocolate) and alcohol in the evenings. Hot milk drinks may be beneficial. Caffeine is a stimulant (Brown *et al.* 1995) and remains active in the body for three to five hours (Ancoli-Israel 1997). Restless leg syndrome and nocturnal myoclonus may be exacerbated by caffeine.

- Address excessive hunger or fullness at bedtime. A light supper or snacks on waking may be beneficial.

- Avoid the drinking of large quantities of liquid in the evening. Elderly people, especially those with heart failure, produce most of their urine when in the lying position.

- Maintain a reasonable weight for the person. Obesity increases daytime fatigue and sleep apnoea.

- Arrange a medication review to report on the drugs which the person is taking and which could cause insomnia, dreaming or nightmares.

- Be sensitive to individual requirements for sleep times. However, going to bed and arising at the same time each day helps to establish a sleep pattern. Consider lifetime patterns of sleep such as experienced by farmers or shift workers, especially in people with dementia.

- Discourage long periods of wakefulness in bed for ambulatory residents. The provision of TV, reading or meals in bed may be counterproductive.

- Trying to force sleep may not be helpful. If wakeful during the night, encourage the person to leave bed and perform a relaxing activity until drowsy. Suggest a separate environment for such activities.

- Consider the effects of daytime naps. In some cases daytime naps may reduce evening tiredness, but some elderly people function better during the day and sleep better at night with a daytime nap (Asplund 1996).

- Provide relaxing activities such as TV, videos, discussion groups or craft activities after the evening meal to delay bedtime and improve sleep.

- A back rub and use of relaxation tapes have been found to promote sleep (McDowell et al. 1998).

- Encourage routine exercise, but not too close to bedtime.

- Provide mental stimulation during the day.

- Provide a comfortable sleeping environment.

- Night-lights may provide reassurance to some, but in other cases may tend to disrupt sleep.

- Bright light therapy has been claimed to normalize disturbed sleep and reduce agitation and sundowning in elderly people with dementia. (Mishima et al. 1994; Satlin et al. 1992). This involves interventions such as using a 2000-lux visor worn for 30 minutes while watching TV each evening (Cooke et al.

1998). A more recent review of the literature has suggested that there is insufficient evidence to assess the value of bright light therapy in people with dementia (Forbes *et al.* 2004). Increased exposure to daylight, which promotes melatonin production, has been claimed to improve sleep patterns (Campbell, Dawson and Anderson 1993).

- Offer paracetamol to enhance comfort.

- Avoid the regular use of sleeping pills. Side-effects are numerous and patients become dependent on their use, while their hypnotic benefit rapidly wears off. Such therapy, when necessary, must be rationed to preserve effect.

7

# Importance of teamwork, training and support

Teamwork, training and support are fundamental to care in the residential aged-care environment.

- Share information relevant to the person's needs and successful interventions amongst all members of the care team. Occasionally a staff member will come across some simple technique to which the person responds, and not realize that no-one else is aware of this technique.

- Involve the family as part of the team in determining techniques for addressing stress in residential care.

- Ancillary as well as hands-on care staff should benefit from special training to develop skills and self-confidence in the care of people with dementia and the prevention and management of stress-related behaviours. Many carers may not understand the relationship of the cognitive, behavioural and psychological symptoms they observe to the diagnosis of dementia, the time course of dementia or the presentation of lost and retained capabilities. Education should include developing an understanding of the symptoms that are present in the person for whom they care (Paton *et al.* 2004). Education and training has been shown to be effective in reducing resident aggression and enhancing nursing home safety (Fitzwater and Gates 2002). Training caregivers in sensitivity to non-verbal communication can reduce symptoms in patients and improve the psychological wellbeing in caregivers as well (Magai, Cohen and Gomberg 2002). Furthermore, education for all staff working in residential care settings has the potential to prevent residents with dementia from requiring more specialized (and expensive) care services (Brodaty, Draper and Low 2003).

- If all carers cannot be offered formal training, utilize one specially trained carer as a consultant.

- The frequent association of agitation with psychosis and depression in people with dementia suggests that specialist psychogeriatric services need to be available to nursing homes and smaller facilities (Brodaty *et al.* 2001).

- Caring for people with dementia can be rewarding yet demanding and stressful. Ensure all the care staff are receiving support.

The Carer's Proverb

'I may not be able to
renew the body
or restore the mind,
but what I can do
is rekindle the spirit.'

# References

Acton, G., Mayhew, P. and Hopkins, B. *et al.* (1999) 'Communicating with individuals with dementia: The impaired person's perspective.' *Journal of Gerontological Nursing 25*, 6–13.

Alessi, C.A., Yoon, E.J. and Schnelle, J.F. *et al.* (1999) 'A randomized trial of a combined physical activity and environmental intervention in nursing home residents: Do sleep and agitation improve?' *Journal of the American Geriatrics Society 47*, 784–791.

Algase, D.L. (1993) 'Wandering: Assessment and intervention.' In P.A. Szwabo and G.T. Grossberg (eds) *Problem Behaviors in Long-term Care: Recognition, Diagnosis and Treatment.* New York: Springer Publishing, pp.163–175.

Algase, D.L., Beck, C. and Kolanowski, A. *et al.* (1996) 'Need-driven dementia-compromised behaviour: An alternative view of disruptive behaviour.' *American Journal of Alzheimer's Disease 11*, 10, 12–19.

Allan, K. (ed.) (1994) *Wandering.* Stirling: Dementia Services Development Centre, University of Stirling.

Allen-Burge, R., Stevens, A.B. and Burgio, L.D. (1999) 'Effective behavioral interventions for decreasing dementia-related challenging behavior in nursing homes.' *International Journal of Geriatric Psychiatry 14*, 213–232.

American Psychiatric Association (1997) 'Practice guidelines for the treatment of patients with Alzheimer's disease and other dementias of late life.' *American Journal of Psychiatry 154*, Suppl 5, s.1–39.

Ancoli-Israel, S. (1997) 'Sleep problems in older adults: Putting myths to bed.' *Geriatrics 52*, 20–28.

Anderson, M.A., Wendler, M.C and Congdon, J.C. (1998) 'Entering the world of dementia. CNA interventions for nursing home residents.' *Journal of Gerontological Nursing 24*, 31–37.

Archibald, C. (1994) 'Food as an activity.' In *Food and Nutrition in the Care of People with Dementia.* Stirling: Dementia Services Development Centre, University of Stirling.

Asplund, R. (1996) 'Daytime sleepiness and napping amongst the elderly in relation to somatic health and medical treatment.' *Journal of International Medicine 239*, 261–267.

Bachman, D. (1992) 'Sleep disorders with ageing: Evaluation and treatment.' *Geriatrics 47*, 53–61.

Baker J. (2001) 'Life-story books for the elderly mentally ill.' *International Journal of Language and Communication Disorders 36*, Suppl 36, s.185–187.

Banazak, D.A. (1996) 'Difficult dementia: Six steps to control problem behaviors.' *Geriatrics 51*, 36–42.

Barratt, J. (1999) 'Snacks as nutritional support in dementia care.' *Nursing Times 95*, 46–47.

Beattie, E.R., Algase, D.L. and Song, J. (2004) 'Keeping wandering nursing home residents at the table: Improving food intake using a behavioral communication intervention.' *Aging and Mental Health 8*, 109–116.

Beck, C.K. (1998) 'Psychosocial and behavioral interventions for Alzheimer's disease patients and their families.' *American Journal of Geriatric Psychiatry 6*, Suppl 1, s.41–48.

Beck, C.K. and Shue, V.M. (1994) 'Interventions for treating disruptive behavior in demented elderly people.' *Nursing Clinics of North America 29*, 143–155.

Beck, C.K. and Vogelpohl, T.S. (1999) 'Problematic vocalizations in institutionalized individuals with dementia.' *Journal of Gerontological Nursing 25*, 17–26.

Bergman-Evans, B. (2004) 'Beyond the basics. Effects of the Eden Alternative Model on quality of life issues.' *Journal of Gerontological Nursing 30*, 27–34.

Billing, N. (1996) 'Management of agitation in nursing home patients: Treatment options.' *Drugs and Aging 9*, 93–100.

Bird, M. (1998) 'Clinical use of preserved learning capacity in dementia.' *Australian Journal of Ageing 17*, 161–166.

Bliwise, D.L. (2000) 'Circadian rhythms and agitation.' *Journal of International Psychogeriatrics 12*, Suppl 1, s.143–146.

Bourgeois, M. (1990) 'Enhancing conversation skills in Alzheimer's disease using a prosthetic memory aid.' *Journal of Applied Behavioural Science 23*, 29–42.

Brawley, E.C. (1998) 'Environment – A silent partner in caring'. In M. Kaplan and S.B. Hoffman (eds) *Behaviours in Dementia: Best Practices for Successful Management.* Baltimore NJ: Health Professionals Press, pp.107–124.

Brocker, P., Benhamidat, T. and Benoit, M. *et al.* (2003) 'Nutritional status and Alzheimer's disease: Preliminary results of the REAL.FR study.' *Revista Medica Internationale 24*, Suppl 3, s.314–318.

Brodaty, H., Draper, B.M. and Low, L.F. (2003) 'Behavioural and psychological symptoms of dementia: A seven-tiered model of service delivery.' *Medical Journal of Australia 178*, 231–234.

Brodaty, H., Draper, B. and Saab, D. *et al.* (2001) 'Psychosis, depression and behavioural disturbances in Sydney nursing home residents: Prevalence and predictors.' *International Journal of Geriatric Psychiatry 16*, 504–512.

Brown, S.L., Salive, M.C. and Pahor, M. *et al.* (1995) 'Occult caffeine as a source of sleep problems in an older population.' *Journal of the American Geriatrics Society 43*, 860–864.

Buckwalter, K.C. (1995) 'What successful approaches do you use in dealing with sexually aggressive patients/residents? Your turn.' *Journal of Gerontological Nursing 21*, 51–52.

Burgener, S.C., Shimer, R. and Murrell, L. (1993) 'Expressions of individuality in cognitively impaired elders. Need for self assessment and care.' *Journal of Gerontological Nursing 19*, 13–22.

Burgio, L. and Fisher, S. (2000) 'Application of psychosocial interventions for treating behavioral and psychological symptoms of dementia.' *Journal of International Psychogeriatrics 12*, Suppl 1, s.351–358.

Burgio, L.D., Allen-Burge, R. and Roth, D.L, et al. (2001) 'Come talk with me: Improving communication between nursing assistants and nursing home residents during care routines.' *Gerontologist 41*, 449–460.

Burgio, L.D., Scilley, K. and Hardin, J. et al. (1996) 'Environmental "white noise". An intervention for verbally agitated nursing home residents.' *Journal of Gerontology B Psychological Science and Social Science 51*, 354–373.

Burns, A., Ballard, C. and Holmes C. (2002) 'Sensory stimulation in dementia.' *British Medical Journal 325*, 1312–1313.

Campbell, S.S., Dawson, D. and Anderson, M.W. (1993) 'Alleviation of sleep maintenance insomnia with timed exposure to bright light.' *Journal of the American Geriatrics Society 41*, 829–836.

Cariaga, J., Burgio, L. and Flynn, W. et al. (1991) 'A controlled study of disruptive vocalizations among geriatric residents in nursing homes.' *Journal of the American Geriatrics Society 39*, 501–507.

Caron, W. and Goetz, D.R. (1998) 'A biopsychosocial perspective on behavioral problems in Alzheimer's disease.' *Geriatrics 53*, Suppl 1, s.56–60.

Chapman, A. and Kerr, D. (eds) (1996) *A Person-centered Approach to Care.* Stirling: Dementia Services Development Centre, University of Stirling.

Clare, L., Wilson, B.A. and Carter, G. et al. (2000) 'Intervening with everyday memory problems in dementia of Alzheimer type: An errorless learning approach.' *Journal of Clinical and Experimental Neuropsychology 22*, 132–146.

Clark, M.E., Lipe, A.W. and Bilbrey, M. (1998) 'The use of music to decrease aggressive behaviours in people with dementia.' *Journal of Gerontological Nursing 24*, 10–17.

Cohen-Mansfield, J. (1989) 'Agitation in the elderly.' *Geriatric Psychiatry 19*, 101–113.

Cohen-Mansfield, J. (1999) 'Measurement of inappropriate behavior associated with dementia. Using direct observation, caregiver ratings, or technological devices for assessment to help understand causes of problem behavior.' *Journal of Gerontological Nursing 25*, 42–51.

Cohen-Mansfield, J. and Billing, N. (1986) 'Agitated behaviours in the elderly: A conceptual review.' *Journal of the American Geriatrics Society 34*, 722–727.

Cohen-Mansfield, J., Werner, P. and Marx, M.S. (1990) 'Screaming in nursing home residents.' *Journal of the American Geriatrics Society 38*, 785–792.

Connelly, J.E. (1999) '"Back-rub!": Reflections on touch.' *The Lancet 354*, Suppl 3, s.1112–1114.

Cooke, K.M., Kreydatus, M.A. and Atherton, A. *et al.* (1998) 'The effects of evening light exposure on the sleep of elderly women expressing sleep complaints.' *Journal of Behavioral Medicine 21*, 103–114.

Coulson, J.S. (2000) 'Shhh: An expert system for the management of clients with vocally disruptive behaviours in dementia.' *Educational Gerontology 26*, 401–408.

Dawson, P., Kline, K. and Wiancko, D.C. *et al.* (1986) 'Preventing excess disability in patients with Alzheimer's disease.' *Geriatric Nursing 6*, 298–301.

Deutsch, L.H. and Rovner, B.W. (1991) 'Agitation and other noncognitive abnormalities in Alzheimer's disease.' *Psychiatric Clinics of North America 14*, 341–351.

Doyle, C., Zapparoni, T. and O'Connor, D. *et al.* (1997) 'Efficiency of psychosocial treatments for noisemaking in severe dementia.' *International Psychogeriatrics 9*, 405–422.

Draper, B., Brodaty, H. and Low, L.F. (2002) 'Types of nursing home residents with self-destructive behaviours: Analysis of the Harmful Behaviours Scale.' *International Journal of Geriatric Psychiatry 17*, 670–675.

Dyck, G. (1997) 'Management of geriatric behavior problems.' *Psychiatric Clinics of North America 20*, 165–180.

Espino, D.V., Jules-Bradley, C.A. and Johnston, C.L. *et al.* (1998) 'Diagnostic approach to the confused elderly patient.' *American Family Physician 57*, 1358–1366.

Eustace, A., Kidd, N. and Greene, E. *et al.* (2001) 'Verbal aggression in Alzheimer's disease. Clinical, functional and neuropsychological correlates.' *International Journal of Geriatric Psychiatry 16*, 858–861.

Feil, N. (1998) *Validation, the Feil Method: How to Help the Disorientated Old-old.* Cleveland, OH: Edward Feil Productions.

Feldt, K.S., Warne, M.A. and Ryden, M.B. (1998) 'Examining pain in aggressive cognitively impaired older adults.' *Journal of Gerontological Nursing 24*, 14.

Fitzwater, E.L. and Gates, D.M. (2002) 'Testing an intervention to reduce assaults on nursing assistants in nursing homes: A pilot study.' *Geriatric Nursing 23*, 18–23.

Folks, D.G. and Burke, W.J. (1998) 'Sedative hypnotics and sleep.' *Clinical Geriatric Medicine 14*, 67–87.

Folstein, M.F., Folstein, S.E. and McHugh, P.R. (1975) '"Mini-Mental State": A practical method for grading the cognitive state of patients for the clinician.' *Journal of Psychiatric Research 12*, 189–198.

Forbes, D., Morgan, D.G. and Bangma, J. *et al.* (2004) 'Light therapy for managing sleep, behaviour, and mood disturbances in dementia.' *Cochrane Database System Review*, 2:CD003946.

Gerdner, L.A. (2000) 'Music, art, and recreational therapies in the treatment of behavioral and psychological symptoms of dementia.' *Journal of International Psychogeriatrics 12*, Suppl 1, s.359–366.

Gibson, F. (ed.) (1991) *The Lost Ones: Recovering the Past to Help their Present.* Stirling: Dementia Services Development Centre, University of Stirling.

Gwynther, L.P. (1985) *Care of Alzheimer's Patients: A Manual for Nursing Home Staff.* Nashville TN: American Health Care Association and Alzheimer's Disease and Related Disorders Association.

Haddad, P.M. and Benbow, S.M. (1993) 'Sexual problems associated with dementia: Part 1. Problems and their consequences.' *International Journal of Geriatric Psychiatry 8*, 547–551.

Haffmans, P.M., Sival, R.C., Lucius, S.A. and Cats, Q. *et al.* (2001) 'Bright light therapy and melatonin in motor restless behaviour in dementia: A placebo controlled study.' *International Journal of Geriatric Psychiatry 16*, 106–110.

Hall, G.R. (1994) 'Caring for people with Alzheimer's disease using the conceptual model of progressively lowered stress threshold in the clinical setting.' *Nursing Clinics of North America 29*, 129–141.

Hall, G.R. and Buckwalter, K.C. (1991) 'Whole disease care planning: Fitting the program to the client with Alzheimer's dementia.' *Journal of Gerontological Nursing 17*, 38–41.

Hall, G., Kirschling, M. and Todd, S. (1986) 'Sheltered freedom – an Alzheimer's Unit in an ICF.' *Geriatric Nursing 7*, 132–136.

Hart, D.J., Craig, D. and Compton, S.A. *et al.* (2003) 'A retrospective study of the behavioural and psychological symptoms of mid and late phase Alzheimer's disease.' *International Journal of Geriatric Psychiatry 18*, 1037–1042.

Herrmann, N. (2001) 'Recommendations for the management of behavioral and psychological symptoms of dementia.' *Canadian Journal of Neurological Science 28*, Suppl 1, s.96–107.

Hoeffer, B., Rader, J. and McKenzie, D. *et al.* (1997) 'Reducing aggressive behaviour during bathing cognitively impaired nursing home residents.' *Journal of Gerontological Nursing 23*, 16–23.

Hoffman, S.B. (1998a) 'Innovations in behaviour management.' In M. Kaplan and S.B. Hoffman (eds) *Behaviours in Dementia: Best Practices for Successful Management.* Baltimore NJ: Health Professionals Press, pp.13–23.

Hoffman, S.B. (1998b) 'Nurturing.' In M. Kaplan and S.B. Hoffman (eds) *Behaviours in Dementia: Best Practices for Successful Management.* Baltimore NJ: Health Professionals Press, pp.63–70.

Holden, U. and Chapman, A. (eds) (1994) *'Wait a Minute!' A Practical Guide on Challenging Behaviour and Aggression for Staff Working with Individuals who have Dementia.* Stirling: Dementia Services Development Centre, University of Stirling.

Holmes, C., Hopkins, V. and Hensford, C. *et al.* (2002) 'Lavender oil as a treatment for agitated behaviour in severe dementia: A placebo controlled study.' *International Journal of Geriatric Psychiatry 17*, 305–308.

Hutchinson, S., Leger-Krall, S. and Wilson, H.S. (1996) 'Toileting. A behavioural challenge in Alzheimer's dementia care.' *Journal of Gerontological Nursing 22*, 19–27.

Hwang, J.P., Tsai, S.J. and Yang, C.H. *et al.* (1999) 'Persecutory delusions in dementia.' *Journal of Clinical Psychiatry 60,* 550–553.

Johansson, K., Zingmark, K. and Norberg, A. (1999) 'Narratives of care providers concerning picking behavior among institutionalized dementia sufferers.' *Geriatric Nursing 20,* 29–32.

Kaasalainen, S., Middleton, J. and Knezacek, S. *et al.* (1998) 'Pain and cognitive status in the institutionalized elderly.' *Journal of Gerontological Nursing 24,* 24–31.

Katz, I.R. (2000) 'Agitation, aggressive behavior, and catastrophic reactions.' *Journal of International Psychogeriatrics 12,* Suppl 1, s.119–124.

Kitwood, T. (1997) *Dementia Reconsidered: The Person Comes First.* Bristol PA: Open University Press.

Kydd, P. (2001) 'Using music therapy to help a client with Alzheimer's disease adapt to long-term care.' *American Journal of Alzheimer's Disease and Other Dementias 16,* 103–108.

Landreville, P., Bordes, M. and Dicaire, L. *et al.* (1998) 'Behavioral approaches for reducing agitation in residents of long-term care facilities: Critical review and suggestions for future research.' *International Psychogeriatrics 10,* 397–419.

Lehninger, F.W., Ravindran, V. and Stewart, J.T. (1998) 'Management strategies for problem behaviors in the patient with dementia.' *Geriatrics 53,* 55–75.

Lichtenberg, P.A. and MacNeill, S.E. (1998) 'Role of the mental health consultant in behaviour management.' In M. Kaplan and S.B. Hoffman (eds) *Behaviours in Dementia: Best Practices for Successful Management.* Baltimore NJ: Health Professionals Press, pp.71–87.

Low, L.F., Brodaty, H. and Draper, B. (2002) 'A study of premorbid personality and behavioural and psychological symptoms of dementia in nursing home residents.' *International Journal of Geriatric Psychiatry 17,* 779–783.

Magai, C., Cohen, C.I. and Gomberg, D. (2002) 'Impact of training dementia caregivers in sensitivity to nonverbal emotion signals.' *International Psychogeriatrics 14,* 25–38.

Malone, L. (ed.) (1996) *Mealtimes and Dementia.* Stirling: Dementia Services Development Centre, University of Stirling.

Mansdorf, I.J., Calapai, P. and Caselli, L. *et al.* (1999) 'Reducing psychotropic medication usage in nursing home residents: The effects of behaviorally oriented psychotherapy.' *Behavioral Therapist 22,* 21–39.

Mant, A. and Bearpark, H. (1990) 'Management of insomnia.' *Australian Prescriber 13,* 51–54.

Matteson, M.A., Linton, F. and Linton, A. (1996) 'Wandering behaviors in institutionalized people with dementia.' *Journal of Gerontological Nursing 22,* 39–44.

Mayers, K. and Griffin, M. (1990) 'The play project: Use of stimulus objects with demented patients.' *Journal of Gerontological Nursing 16,* 32–37.

McDowell, J.A., Mion, L.C. and Lydon, T.J. *et al.* (1998) 'A nonpharmacologic sleep protocol for hospitalized older patients.' *Journal of the American Geriatrics Society 46,* 700–705.

McGillivray, T. and Marland, G.R. (1999) 'Assisting demented patients with feeding: Problems in a ward environment.' A review of the literature. *Journal of Advanced Nursing 29*, 608–614.

Meares, S. and Draper, B. (1999) 'Treatment of vocally disruptive behaviour of multifactorial aetiology.' *International Journal of Geriatric Psychiatry 14*, 285–290.

Meins, W., Frey, A. and Thiesemann, R. (1998) 'Premorbid personality traits in Alzheimer's disease: Do they predispose to noncognitive behavioral symptoms?' *International Psychogeriatrics 10*, 369–378.

Menon, A.S., Gruber-Baldini, A.L. and Hebel, J.R. *et al.* (2001) 'Relationship between aggressive behaviors and depression among nursing home residents with dementia.' *International Journal of Geriatric Psychiatry 6*, 139–146.

Mintzer, J.E. and Brawman-Mintzer, O. (1996) 'Agitation as a possible expression of generalized anxiety disorder in demented elderly patients: Toward a treatment approach.' *Journal of Clinical Psychiatry 57*, Suppl 17, s.55–63.

Mintzer, J.E., Hoernig, K.S. and Mirski, D.F. (1998) 'Treatment of agitation in patients with dementia.' *Clinics of Geriatric Medicine 14*, 147–175.

Mishima, K., Okawa, M. and Hishikawa Y. *et al.* (1994) 'Morning bright light therapy for sleep and behavior disorders in elderly patients with dementia.' *Acta Psychiatrica Scandanavia 89*, 1–7.

Morley, J.E. and Miller, D.K. (1993) 'Behavioural concomitants of common medical disorders.' In P.A. Szwabo and G.T. Grossberg (eds) *Problem Behaviors in Long-term Care: Recognition, Diagnosis and Treatment.* New York: Springer Publishing, pp.97–109.

Namazi, K.H. and Johnson, B.D. (1996) 'Issues related to behavior and the physical environment: Bathing cognitively impaired patients.' *Geriatric Nursing 17*, 234–239.

Neufeld, R.R., Libow, L.S. and Foley, W.J. *et al.* (1999) 'Restraint reduction reduces serious injuries to nursing home residents.' *Journal of the American Geriatrics Society 47*, 1202–1207.

Orsulic-Jeras, S., Judge, K.S. and Camp, C.J. (2000) 'Montessori-based activities for long-term care residents with advanced dementia: Effects on engagement and affect.' *Gerontologist 40*, 107–111.

Palsson, S., Johannson, B. and Berg, S. *et al.* (2000) 'A population study on the influence of depression on neuropsychological functioning in 85-year-olds.' *Acta Psychiatrica Scandanavia 101*, 185–193.

Passafiume, D., Di Giacomo, D. and Giubilei F. (2000) 'Reading latency of words and nonwords in Alzheimer's patients.' *Cortex 36*, 293–298.

Paton, J., Johnston, K. and Katona, C. *et al.* (2004) 'What causes problems in Alzheimer's disease: Attributions by caregivers.' A qualitative study. *International Journal of Geriatric Psychiatry 19*, 527–532.

Peterson, A. and Lantz, M.S. (2001) 'Is it Alzheimer's? Neuropsychological testing helps to clarify diagnostic puzzle.' *Geriatrics 56*, 58–59.

Philo, S.W., Richie, M.F. and Kaas, M.J. (1996) 'Inappropriate sexual behaviour.' *Journal of Gerontological Nursing 22*, 17–22.

Potkins, D., Myint, P. and Bannister, C. *et al.* (2003) 'Language impairment in dementia: Impact on symptoms and care needs in residential homes.' *International Journal of Geriatric Psychiatry 18*, 1002–1006.

Rapp, M.S., Flint, A.J., Herrmann, N. and Proulx, G.B. (1992) 'Behavioural disturbances in the demented elderly: Phenomenology, pharmacotherapy and behavioural management.' *Canadian Journal of Psychiatry 37*, 651–657.

Raskind, M.A. (1999) 'Evaluation and management of aggressive behaviour in the elderly demented patient.' *Journal of Clinical Psychiatry 60*, Suppl 15, s.45–8.

Reynolds, C., Hock, C.C. and Stack, J. *et al.* (1988) 'The nature and management of sleep–wake disturbance in Alzheimer's dementia.' *Psychopharmacological Bulletin 24*, 43–48.

Roberts, C. (1999) 'Research in brief: The management of wandering in older people with dementia.' *Journal of Clinical Nursing 8*, 322–324.

Rogers, J.C., Holm, M.B. and Burgio, L.D. *et al.* (1999) 'Improving morning care routines of nursing home residents with dementia.' *Journal of the American Geriatrics Society 47*, 1049–1057.

Rubin, E.H., Veiel, L.L. and Kinscherf, D.A. *et al.* (2001) 'Clinically significant depressive symptoms and very mild to mild dementia of the Alzheimer type.' *International Journal of Geriatric Psychiatry 16*, 694–701.

Ryan, E.B., Kennaley, D.E. and Pratt, M.W. *et al.* (2000) 'Evaluations by staff, residents, and community seniors of patronizing speech in the nursing home: Impact of passive, assertive, or humorous responses.' *Psychology and Aging 15*, 272–285.

Ryden, M.B., Bossenmaier, M. and McLauchlan, C. (1991) 'Agressive behaviour in cognitively impaired nursing home residents.' *Nursing and Health, 14*, 87–95.

Satlin, A., Volicer, L. and Ross, V. *et al.* (1992) 'Bright light treatment of behavioral and sleep disturbances in patients with Alzheimer's disease.' *American Journal of Psychiatry 149*, 1028–1032.

Shelkey, M. and Lantz, M. (1998) 'Promoting behavioral alternatives to psychotropic drug use on a dementia special care unit.' Presentation to the American Geriatrics Society Annual General Meeting. *Journal of American Geriatrics Society 46*, Suppl 9, s.96.

Sherratt, K., Thornton, A. and Hatton, C. (2004) 'Emotional and behavioural responses to music in people with dementia: An observational study.' *Aging and Mental Health 8*, 233–241.

Simard, J. (1999) 'Making a positive difference in the lives of nursing home residents with Alzheimer disease: The lifestyle approach.' *Alzheimer Disease and Associated Disorders 13*, Suppl 1, s.67–72.

Skovdahl, K., Kihlgren, A.L. and Kihlgren, M. (2003) 'Different attitudes when handling aggressive behaviour in dementia – Narratives from two caregiver groups.' *Ageing and Mental Health 7*, 277–286.

Sloane, P.D., Davidson, S. and Knight, N. *et al.* (1999) 'Severe disruptive vocalizers.' *Journal of the American Geriatrics Society 47*, 439–445.

Sobel, B.P. (2001) 'Bingo vs. physical intervention in stimulating short-term cognition in Alzheimer's disease patients.' *American Journal of Alzheimer's Disease and Other Dementias 16*, 115–120.

Solomon, K. (1993) 'Behavioural and psychotherapeutic interventions with residents in the long-term care institution.' In P.A. Szwabo and G.T. Grossberg (eds) *Problem Behaviors in Long-term Care: Recognition, Diagnosis and Treatment.* New York: Springer Publishing, pp.147–162.

Spetor, A., Orrell, M. and Davies, S. *et al.* (2000) 'Reality orientation for dementia.' *Cochrane Database System Review*, 2:CD001119.

Swift, M.B., Williams, R.B. and Potter, M.L. (2002) 'Behaviour of nursing home residents.' *Journal of Psychological Nursing 40*, 41–45.

Szwabo, P.A. and Boesch, K.R. (1993) 'Impact of personality and personality disorders in the elderly.' In P.A. Szwabo and G.T. Grossberg (eds) *Problem Behaviors in Long-term Care: Recognition, Diagnosis and Treatment.* New York: Springer Publishing, pp.59–69.

Tariot, P. (1996) 'Treatment strategies for agitation and psychosis in dementia.' *Journal of Clinical Psychiatry 57*, Suppl 14, s.21–29.

Taylor, J.A., Ray, W.H. and Meador, K.G. (1995) *Managing Behavioural Symptoms in Nursing Home Residents. A Manual for Nursing Home Staff. Continuing Education for Nursing Homes in Tennessee.* Nashville TN: Vanderbilt University School of Medicine.

Touhy, T. (2004) 'Dementia, personhood and nursing: Learning from a nursing situation.' *Nursing Science Quarterly 17*, 43–49.

Verhey, F.R.J. and Visser, P.J. (2000) 'Phenomenology of depression in dementia.' *Journal of International Psychogeriatrics 12*, Suppl 1, s.129–134.

Volicer, L., Harper, D.G. and Manning, B.C. *et al.* (2001) 'Sundowning and circadian rhythms in Alzheimer's disease.' *American Journal of Psychiatry 158*, 704–711.

de Vugt, M.E., Stevens, F. and Aalten, P. *et al.* (2004) 'Do caregiver management strategies influence patient behaviour in dementia?' *International Journal of Geriatric Psychiatry 19*, 85–92.

Wick, J. and Reid, C. (1997) 'Defusing violent and aggressive behaviour in the long-term care setting.' *The Consultant Pharmacist 12*, 1064–1070.

Wlosinski, B. and Diaello, L. (2001) 'Treatment of inappropriate sexual behaviour in the cognitively impaired elderly.' Chicago: Lecture. American Society of Consultant Pharmacists 32nd Annual Meeting and Exhibition.

Yakabowich, M. (1990) 'Prescribe with care: The role of laxatives in the treatment of constipation.' *Journal of Gerontological Nursing 16*, 4–11.

Zeisel, J., Silverstein, N.M. and Hyde, J. *et al.* (2003) 'Environmental correlates to behavioral health outcomes in Alzheimer's special care units.' *Gerontologist 43*, 697–711.

# Subject index

# Author index